JAI MATA DI, MY BOOK ON HUMAN WELFARE

RAJESH D SANGHVI

ISBN

Hardcase 979-8-89519-056-2
Paperpack 978-1-63669-501-3

Dedicated to my Guru-Sadhguru Jaggi Vasudevji, my Uncle
Shri. Mahesh P Sanghvi, and my wife Tejal R Sanghvi

Dear Self,

Becoming available to
the Infinite intelligence
of the Creation is the only
way to know life in its
full depth and dimension

May You know
the Bliss of the Divine

love and Blessings

Dear RAJESH D SANGHVI ,

Namaskaram. Hope you are doing well and enjoying your Shambhavi Mahamudra kriya. We're happy to pass along this personal message from Sadhguru and look forward to having you take part in this amazing journey.

You can keep in touch with Sadhguru and Isha through Facebook – thought provoking articles addressing various aspects of life, profound daily quotes, Sadhguru's views on current affairs, insightful and inspiring videos - you can find all this and much more.

"Like" Sadhguru's Facebook page
"Like" Isha Foundation's Facebook page

If you have any questions about your kriya, please write to kriyasupport@ishayoga.org

Hope Inner Engineering has enriched your life and that you continue to nurture the seed planted in you!

Pranam,
Swami Nandaka
swami.nandaka@ishafoundation.org

Dear RAJESH D SANGHVI ,

Namaskaram. Hope your practices are going well. We would like to take this opportunity to welcome you and your family to the Isha Yoga Center in Coimbatore. An uplifting and rejuvenating space for self-transformation consecrated by Sadhguru, set against the beautiful and serene backdrop of Velliangiri foothills, the ashram offers a welcome break from the hustle and bustle of city life, and also a potent atmosphere for inner discoveries.

Meditating in Dhyanalinga, soaking in the Linga Bhairavi's grace, invigorating dips in the Theerthakund and doing your practices in the vibrant Ashram space will leave you drenched in vitality, peace, and the visible glow of a purified body and mind.

On a parallel note, you could take the step of volunteering. This can be in the form of offering this sacred science to your friends and family by sharing your experience with them. Or you might want to experience the Inner Engineering program again as a volunteer. You can also involve yourself in the social outreach projects.

I hope this journey has been enriching and that you will continue to nurture the Shambhavi Mahamudra Kriya. Stay connected and inspired via Facebook, Youtube, Blog.

Pranam,
Swami Nandaka

Contents

Rajesh D Sanghvi, is a Business man by profession, works in own family run Automobile distribution business from more than past two decades. He is a Double post Graduate from London, U.K. where he gained his Degrees. While still in his teens, he read his first Guru's book, Mahatma Gandhi, Bapu, The father of our Nation Bharat! In his Autobiography "The story of my Experiments with Truth". Rajesh beliefs that he learnt his Truth about life and existance from his Great Guru Mahatama Gandhi, who is still a source of inspiration to him, and drives him to pursue Human welfare activities, with absolute selflessness! Swami Vivekananda, came to him, Still further in his college days, he used to hear lectures at Ramkrishamath, delivered by the Disciples of Shri Ramakrishna Paramhansa on shaping the future of our nation, and was Greatly influenced by the Nationalist spirit and Spirituality propounded in his writings, as he read and absorbed the teachings of Swami Vivekananda his Second Guru, who firmly built patriotism and a sense of service to Bharat in him. Meanwhile he got married to Tejal and has two sweet children of his own from her. He feels his wife Tejal was a source of Great support, and Strength in his life, and he feels he owes his various achievements to the love and encouragement provided by her.

It was his wife Tejal who gifted him the DVD's of Ramayana by Ramanand Sagar, which he liked so much, that he saw it 4 times in his life till date! He also went on to see Shri Krishna by Ramanand sagar, apart from the Mahabharata, by B.R. Chopra, which led him to read and absorb the Bhagavat Gita and its teachings, which he continues to read today.

But being a Gujrati-Jain by religion, he was also well versed with the Agama Shastra, Bhagtambar, and other religious teachings of his Jain religion.

His preoccupation and inquisitiveness about religious ways, also lead him to study other religions texts among them the Guru Granth Sahib, the Holy Quran and the Bible.

It was a Great day for Rajesh, when his wife introduced him to Sadhguru Jaggi Vasudevji of Isha foundation, who is his living Third Guru, Sahguru, later in his life. He started his devotion to Sadhguru by watching his various videos available on You tube about a year back, and as he realised, he was amongst a living Guru, he first went on to avail the benefits of Isha's flagship Yoga program inner engineering at a local Isha centre in Hyderabad.

Since then, life has never been the same for Rajesh, as he continued with his love and devotion to his Guru, by visiting his Ashram in Coimbatore, several times and still does, and enrolled himself as an Isha volunteer! He rendered seva at the Ashram to his Guru, in a variety of ways, as he continued to be deeply involved with Isha.

At last Sadhguru noticed the efforts of Rajesh, and his Selflessness nature, and his willingness to go to any extent to help others and devote his life and time for Human welfare and human wellbeing. His Guru's appreciation came in the form of a self-own hand-written letter to Rajesh, expressing his love and blessings to his new disciple, and followed by a second letter, duly inviting his family for a stay at his Ashram in Coimbatore, and to Volunteer for his Isha foundation, both these letter's copies are included in this book written by Rajesh, as a Tribute to his beloved Guru. This was a motivation to Rajesh to move on to the spiritual path, and encourage others to benefit by taking the same path, these letters duly authorize Rajesh to work in the various projects undertaken by Isha foundation as a volunteer!

As Rajesh continued to offer himself to volunteering at the Ashram, by offering Seva on important occasions at the Ashram, like the Sapth Rishi Puja, and work and fundraising efforts to support the Mahashivaratri celebrations 2018 at the Ashram, where he also did his Sadhana on the Occasion. Before he realised, doing his Shambhavi Mahamudra Yoga kriya daily, Rajesh started seeing himself Transformed into a Yogi devoted to the Ashram, as well as serving the cause of Human welfare and human wellbeing, with a tireless, selfless attitude!

His Book richly highlights, a fruit borne out of the collective wisdom imparted to him by his 3 Great Gurus who deeply influenced and shaped his life till date!

His maiden attempt at book writing, was drawn as an inspiration from the teachings of his Guru's, he felt he has a vision and solutions to offer, as he explored and observed the current problems and issues facing our Nation India, the world, our Society, and Generally on an Individual to individual perspective as well!

As he realised, thinking about these problems, he put his mind to work, as to how can we solve these problems, to his pleasant surprise, he was able to find and devise solutions to many problems facing our society, and our world, which he has penned down, with his Prime motive, that being of promoting human welfare and human wellbeing, effective in reducing or eliminating human suffering to a large extent.

He has presented his thoughts in the form of solutions, from quite a new perspective, a fresh look at the common problems plaguing humanity today, most of his thinking process is new to the world, from an experiential, spiritual and practical perspective, which actually addresses and encounters the issues boldly, and are solutions which can be practically implemented, realizing benefits to humanity and our world today, if implemented in our society! A must read for all! And especially made for the law and policy makers in our world!

Here Rajesh addresses issues as diverse as Education, Marriage, to Wars, to Women's welfare, Crime, Medical care, and illness, to poverty, to environmental problems, and many other problems we face as a nation, and in the world, from an entirely new and unknown, unthought off, unconventional perspective, and presents well thought out solutions, which can actually be implemented by the policy by the law makers, and the individuals in their life, to solve many of the issues plaguing our society! A unique opportunity and a must read for all!

Chapter 1

Hindu Religious Education

What is Hindu religious education? Presently in our Nation Bharat, under Article 29 and 30 of the constitution, the miniority religious communities, have been given special rights and protection to impart religious and linguistic education to their children, by establishing their own religious educational institutions, such as the Muslims and the Christians mainly, though the Sikh's the Buddhists, Parsi and Jains, are also classified as minorities under the constitution, but generally, these religions are actually, home grown, and can be treated as broadly part of the Hindu religion, and they too do not have religious educational institutions to teach their religion to their children, they are also considered part of the Hindu community, and can be treated as sects, which have grown out of Hindu religion.

Whilst the Muslims and the Christians, have their own religious institutions to teach their religion to their children, like the Madrasas, and the General Schools, of the Christian communities, named after their religious Saints, the Hindu's do not have any formal provision in the Constitution, to impart Hindu religious education to their children.

Article 30 promises all minorities, both linguistic and religious to establish and administer institutions to impart religious and linguistic education, Article 29, of the constitution provides protection for the religion, culture, and language of these minorities. The institutions so established, have freedom to operate and impart education to serve the purpose of their interest as a community.

However, there is no such provision for imparting religious or linguistic education for the majority community in our constitution, this must be, because the writers of the constitution must have felt, that the majority community will attend to their needs on their own, and care for their own interest, being the majority community.

The present scenario is such that, though there are some very small Hindu religious institutions, imparting some religious education, that too the religious teachings of some saints, of Hindu Origin, to their followers, there is however, no formal Institution which imparts Hindu Religious education to the children in an established and administered manner.

The schools we have currently, is based on western concept, which has been established in our nation, by the British, we get to see British literature like Shakespeare, British poetry, British Prose, and the sciences being taught to the children, such as maths, physics, chemistry, medicines, technology, computers, history, economics, geography etc.

Whilst we need the sciences to be taught to children, as a necessity, and they are good, but the imparting of British culture in our schools, shows that, we have completely ignored our own culture and teaching our own Indian literature, leave alone Hindu religious education.

I will draw out the list, which is a part of what is missing in our schools, The Vedas, the Puranas, the Upanishads are not taught to our children. Our most important religious book-The Bhagwat Gita is not taught. The Agam Shastra, which is the Science of building Temples is not taught. The Stories of our Religious Gods and Goddesses, Shiva, the 9 Mataji's, Ganesha, Krishna, Bramha, Vishnu and the entire

Cosmic order of our God's and Goddesses, are a Subject of our Children to grow up listening, The Patanjali Yoga Sutras are not Taught. The Epics of Ramayana and Mahabharata are not taught. The Four Yoga's taught by Swami Vivekananda are not taught, Giana Yoga, Karma Yoga, Bhakti Yoga, Raja Yoga are not taught. Indian Home-Grown Poetry is not taught. The Knowledge of the Yugas are not given.

The knowledge of the observance of Bhramacharya is not taught, and most importantly, the Science of Yoga and Dhayana is not taught, which is vital for the success of the child, to gain maturity and consciousness. This is the Greatest gift or contribution of Bharat to the world, and it is not taught formally in Bharat itself!

The Science of Martial arts Kalari, which was invented by Bharat, and then absorbed by other countries, like China and Japan, and given a different name there, is more famous in our world, than the Origin of Martial arts Kalari, which is forgotten in our own country, except in a few institutions, to name Isha foundation.

The ancient Science of Ayurveda, the natural cure, is present in our country, but most of it is lost, need to be taught to our children.

Our own home-Grown religions to name Buddhism, Jainism, The Sikh religion, which are a part of the Hindu fold, these religions teachings are not taught. The Teachings of Buddha, The Teachings of the Jain Tirthankaras', Bhagwan Mahavir, The Teachings of Guru Nanak and Guru Gobind Singh are not taught to our Children.

The sacred language of Sanskrit, the origin of all languages in the world, is all but forgotten in Bharat, the place of its Origin. The Chinese have preserved their own language, so have the Japanese, the Koreans, the Arabic, the French, the Italians, the Russians, but our own nation have not preserved it's own Sacred language-Sanskrit. Knowing Sanskrit will open all the ancient scripts and books of Bharat, and children knowing Sanskrit can read and learn about our own Hindu Religion in its original form the Sanskrit scripts.

There are many Saints and their lineages in Bharat, like Sai Ram, Shankar Mutt, and Sankracharya, Raghavendra Swami, etc.. their life and their teachings are not taught.

The True story of our Freedom Struggle, and the Heroes who laid down their life's for our Bharat is not taught, there were many Famous Kings and Queens, their Dynasties, there were many famous personalities from Ancient Bharat to the nearer present, about them noting is taught.

For example Sardar Vallah bhai patel, and his contribution to shaping India, K.B. Hedgewar the Founder of RSS or Rashritiya Sewak Sangh, and the RSS lineage and Great contribution to our nation building, Subhas Chandra Bose and his famous independence army, The King Ashoka, and his story, on whom the Ashok Chakra is based, our national emblem, The Great Women of Bharat, Rani Laxmi Bai, Mira Bai, Sarojini Devi Naidu, Raja Harishchandra, Etc.. The list is very big.. the story of such famous people of Bharat, is yet to be told to and inspired to the Children of Bharat.

There are no books meant for children narrating this and teaching Sanskrit, or Kalari, which is the True Indian Heritage, this is part of Hindu Religious Education to be taught to our Children, all missing!

One way to start Hindu religious education is to establish Hindu religious educational institutions, and administer them to our children, where the practical Sciences like Maths, Physics, Chemistry, Medicine, Technology, Computers, etc is also taught, apart from Yoga,

Dhayana, Kalari Martial arts, Sanskrit, and the Ancient Sciences, Heritage and Culture of Bharat is Taught.

A Second an easy method would be to introduce this education in all Government Schools, where for Muslim and Christian children, learning this Hindu Religious Education, can be left Optional. It would of interest to note that of the total number of Schools, 90% of all Schools and Colleges in India are Government run, so introducing them there, would serve to cover 90% of Children studying in India, and the rest 10% of schools which are private schools, will follow the example of Government Schools, and later can be made Mandatory for them also. This way, our Hindu Religious education can be imparted, in a Successful and scaled up fashion, with quicker results for our Bharat.

Another note, the Sports needs to be given prominence in our Government Schools, physical fitness is very important to building the personality of our children. Secondly, the NCC (The National Cadet Corps), training needs to be made compulsory for all children both in Government and Private, for the Children to be exposed to the Army, Navy and Airforce Training, which will instill some discipline and order in our Sweet Children, and get them oriented to the defence forces of our Bharat!

Doing these changes and Introducing Hindu Religious Education, will ensure, the success of our Children as Citizens of Bharat and of the world, making them proud of our nation, and starting their life's with consciousness and maturity, and the pace of success and development of our nation will definitely happen at a Galloping speed! Imagine how fast we move in our 21st Century, in the right and responsible manner. It is vital to the future of Bharat!

Since Currently Hindu religious education is missing now, formally for our Children, to some Children it comes by chance, this knowledge, or by accident, through self acquisition and persual of this, and may be sometimes, more significantly, whatever they can get from their parents, otherwise they have no formal guidance, and go by default to the nearly British format schools and colleges in our Bharat, with no religious or Spirituality, and fail in life, due to ignorance, and lack of consciousness of the truth about life, and the true nature of our existence, which would come naturally, if they were to be imparted Hindu religious education! May God bless the children of Bharat, and through this article, the Government Authorities take steps towards imparting Hindu religious and linguistic education!

Chapter 2

Living Matajis Amidst Us, The Superior Form of Humans Amongst Us

If there is anything worth admiring in us humans, but naturally, that share of admiration goes to the superior and subtler form of creation in us humans, the other half- the finer sex women!

It is said that God first created man, and then a little later he created women, after checking on the faults he found in man, his first creation, as he was obsessed with creating perfection, and then he created women, the far superior version of humans!

I would like to state some words, on the status of women in our society, they enjoy at present, and what it should be ideally!

Obviously, God worked hard, in his second project! That is the reason a man is never a match to a woman! Let us see how, first, they look better, we describe them as beautiful, wonderful, lovely! That's fine, automatically, our vocabulary of words, needed those changes!

Well, it is no secret that, generally, women have a superior intellect than men! It does not go far to say, they are wiser and smarter as well to men!

One of their greatest strengths is that they have an almost unbelievable capacity to bear pain and hardship, and endurance and the capacity to bear the brunt of the effort needed for our human species to survive. They are endowed with endless strength, to the extent, that we honour them, with by calling them the source of power, all power in humans-Shakti, we never doubt the fact, or tire when we say, that behind every man's success, the reason is the handiwork of a woman!

Let us examine, the personality of women, well the first thing, to start with, the continuation of our human species is through the difficult process of birth, we take for granted, and the creator handed over this responsibility to the fairer sex, amongst us! They bear and carry the child for nine months, then the painful process of human birth happens, their duty continues, as the baby is fed by them, whilst doing their other duties in the home, providing the much needed nourishment, and the safety net which in part is the milk, giving the strength to the child to survive all the dreadful infections, and building the immunity of the child in turn.

The vital task of caring and giving the child the first experience of love in this world, again the women handle with ease, as it is but second nature to them! Well, this talent or ability in us as men needs to be acquired by our own efforts and can never be equal to that of women! The men amongst us need to work hard to gain this reputation of soft nature, like women! This is the reason the children first belong to women, by heart and mind before the man!

We foolishly never realise the important role women play, even as a home maker, they do all the work in the home without complaining, from the most important and vital task of cooking the food, and cleaning the home, caring for the children, caring for the older generation, living with you as well as your parents, to shopping for the home, seeing to it that none of the resources of the home go to waste, be it money or material, to teaching and helping your children at their studies, to taking care of you and meeting your unreasonable demands, but always providing you the best practical advice, taking care of the household expenses, to taking the responsibility to call for repairs to anything causing any discomfort, all this she does, without batting an eyelid!

An important fact that we are aware of but take for granted by the women of the home, which I am sure all have experienced, is that, although the woman of the home, makes you happy by cooking delicious food, she herself eats her meal, after serving each member of the family, you tell her to eat with you, she doesn't listen to you, out of your concern for her, and she replies, and sometimes tells lies, saying that she has eaten already! As she continues to overfeed all the members of the family, with the delicious food she has cooked for the entire family! It is only later it occurs to you, that she may have not had her food at all! At the back of your mind, as you go to sleep with the family, fully fed, and she willingly goes to bed hungry for the day, if the food is exhausted after the family eats! So, she is the one who cooks the food for you, feeds you and is the one who goes to sleep hungry at night! This is a God-like quality of a woman, I pray too with a sense of shame, as despite making my best efforts, I have not been able to discourage this practice of my woman!

So, the woman as a homemaker is no small thing, which we take for granted, for a man to accomplish these feats, day after day, all throughout life, is impossible, I would think a man would not succeed as a homemaker, by lasting for even a week in a homemaker's multirole task! I know I speak the truth in this!

Then in the modern era, of our times, the women of today are highly educated, so the girl child is usually the topper in the school too, and that's no surprise! As she turns into an adult, she is very highly capable, and we have so many examples today, they do a much better job at work than men, be it any role, in the government, in banks, as CEO's of big companies, be it multinationals, as leaders, as policemen, now as flight pilots, or jet fighters, or even in the army, as scientists, as heads of state or nations, as spiritual leaders too! Nowhere will you find them lacking; they excel at what they do!

Moreover, these working women, generally, remain as the homemakers also, while carrying out their superb work in our society, and making us feel proud of them, and hold them in awe! And our admiration today!

So then, why do we live in a world, where men feel superior in any way to women? Just for the muscular strength! Well, if they received training, they would excel us in that too! Even among our Indian Gods, Shiva mounts a cow, and Mataji, which is rightly treated as the supreme deity, you know on whom she mounts! A lion, of course!

Well, seeing and realising this truth, I feel disgusted, and my heart pains, at the way the women are treated in India or in our world generally! Looking on them, disgustingly, as objects of sensual pleasure and gratification!

In our modern world today, it is high time we realised and accepted this as the supreme truth, and we need to do something about the sorry state of women in our country, and the world! It is our shame that they do not yet enjoy their rightful place of equality, we owe to them in our society! Well, I feel the time has come, when as gentlemen who now declare, "women first" or "ladies first',' it should not only be in lip service for the sake of courtesy! Women should rightly come first in every walk of life! And play an important role in our society as they are meant to, and this is the right ideal for our society, as our creator intended! This is the best and sensible logic today, in our modern era of women empowerment! I am sure this will create a lot of benefit to our society, under their gentle, giving and capable caring!

Chapter 3

The Elixir of Life – The Three-Step Process to Good Karma. Could Hitler Have Been like Jesus If He Knew How to Be One?

This leads to answering some fundamental questions:
Why do we suffer? How do you end suffering?

A Technical Perspective for Humanity

Not that everybody suffers, but most who do, some way or the other in their life, do so because of a lack of consciousness and awareness about some simple truths about life—they are unaware being ignorant about the true nature of our existence or the reality about life, and the way to live.

This is the sole reason for the suffering of most people in their lives. It is living a life with this ignorance—that is the reason for the suffering of most people.

Now let us have a look at this—we have created a society which is surrounded by conditions, where purely due to ignorance of some simple truths about the basis of our existence, collectively for all, we suffer and make others suffer.

Let us start with children; children may suffer due to their parents and the socio-economic environment in which they are bought up. They are innocent to the ways of life—they do not create their own suffering. Suffering is heaped on them, being unlucky to have such circumstances surrounding them, including their parents who live a life lacking consciousness and awareness.

But once they cross their puberty, the hormones in their body become active, the life they lead after they cross their puberty, this suffering is entirely out of their ignorance or their unwillingness to accept the true nature of our existence.

Generally, after they cross their puberty, nobody is available to guide them or educate them about the reality of life, and they are led by impressions that were wrongly created by what they observe in media, or in others who set a bad example to them.

They are bound by the clutches of their sense organs and tendencies to have sensual pleasures, and let alone knowing about this, they progress into a trap that has been created by the hormones at play in their body, which hijack their intelligence.

So, whose duty is it to tell them the truth? Or show them the methodology of untangling themselves from their predicament? It must be their parents, if they have the knowledge of life, or society, or to whom they come in contact with—their teachers, friends or relatives among them who know the truth and are willing to impart their knowledge, to lead the children out of their suffering, which come from pursuing their sensual pleasures. This way of living prompts them towards living a life without consciousness and awareness, bound by the senses.

I now explain the three guidelines, the three steps that are required for nor only children, but all those who are not living a life of consciousness and awareness and do not know the most basic truths about life, and due to which, they ruin their lives.

Action for Self-Restraint: Once a child crosses puberty, his intelligence is hijacked by his hormones attacking his mind and body. The natural tendency of the body and the mind is to procreate when it has reached this capability. That is to have sex with a member of the opposite sex and give birth. The five senses—the eyes, the ears, the mouth, the nose, the skin and the sex organ—are driven naturally towards gratification of an urgent need programmed by the creator himself-to reproduce to ensure the continuity of the human species, and to ensure their survival by reproduction.

That is the way the creator has designed the body and the mind to function to ensure survival and this tendency is the strongest urge as designed by the creator to have sex. And this is laced with the deepest sensual pleasure arousal in the human, to mask its intended purpose. But the need is to restrain these impulses and to achieve control and subjugate the urge, to serve the real purpose it was intended by the creator. But if this remains unchecked, it will cloud the brain, disable the body and the intelligence and lead the individual to degradation and eventual ruin.

Yes, the need to have sex to reproduce is important, but when you use the sexual urge as a means of sensual gratification of the body and mind, purely for the sake of pleasure, the body and the mind deteriorate in health, the capacity to earn a living diminishes, so deterioration in wealth, the ability for true love vanishes, and the individual's behaviour becomes unsocial, ultimately ruining their lives.

The sexual organ was meant to be used for giving birth, not to serve to derive sensual pleasures. This is how suffering comes to a human.

In society, there is a need for marriage and to have a family, a noble need. But it must happen the right way.

So how do we control and achieve supremacy over the mind and body, after the hormones have led their attack on the brain? It is through self-restraint, by achieving control over the palate (tongue – its tendency to eat food laced to give maximum pleasures to the palate).

Achievement of this is very easy, if this is done at a young age. If this methodology is taught at the right time to the teenager, well, the child needs to consume those items which are not pleasant or is neutral in taste and disallow sense gratification of the tongue or palate, but at the same time, the food chosen to consume is nutritious and causes no harm to the body.

This methodology of weaning away and subjugating and controlling the palate will work towards, gaining perfect control over all the senses and subjugate the tendencies for self-gratification of the body and mind by impulsive tendencies of sensual pleasures.

The minimum period of consumption of such foods needs to cross 9 Months to 1 Year, without having a relapse on the momentary acquisition of sensual pleasures within this period of developing self-control over the body and the mind of the person.

This is not a type of fasting or renunciation. None of that. In fact, fasting over long periods, considered a virtue in many religions, will actually harm the body, as fasting leads to a situation in the stomach, where the stomach being empty, the acids produced in the digestive system, cause harm to the stomach and digestive system, with irreparable damage done to the body.

The foods recommended for consumption in this transformational period are salads, fruits in the raw form, with vegetables either in semi cooked boiled form, or even better, it is worth it, that vegetables are also consumed raw as they come. Additionally, some of the essential ingredients of the food need to include plain milk, a small portion of fatty oils, and some salt-added water to keep the body and mind in top and harmless maintenance condition.

In this food, if you include items which taste that are unpleasant to the palate (tongue) like bitter gourd vegetable and neem leaves, the process of body transformation and achieving self-control will be rapid and the goal achieved sooner and even more perfectly. No cooked food in this duration of time, and sticking to this, with no other type of food.

This does require a certain amount of willpower in the follower of this diet, with this practice, a purification of the body takes place, and the body is also detoxified in the process.

Weight loss is normal, during this vital process of self-restraint practised. I will give you my own example.

Before starting this diet, I was heavily built; I weighed 165 kgs. Once I practised this diet for over a year and a half, my body weight reduced to 64 kgs! I was also practising physical exercise to generate heat in the body during this period! But one underlying advantage of this diet is you not only remain healthy, but you also gain a superior state of health condition.

For everyone, the body constitution differs, as per weight and innate tendencies, however it is very sure to deliver the results expected! But the minimum time for the body's transformation to occur is one year on this diet. This diet will unmask the shroud of sensual pleasures surrounding your body and mind and will effectively neutralise the effects of the hormones which attacked the body and mind, and this will be effective, and this will subjugate the tendencies of the mind and the body, which hijacked our intelligence in the first place itself, perfectly and effectively.

The absolute truth I speak here about control of the palate and its benefits are very clearly stated in religious sacred texts and also taught by Guru's to children.

Action point number 2: The practice of yoga and Dhyana every day to raise the degree of awareness and consciousness to 100%, an appreciable by-product of practising yoga and Dhyana, daily, is a meteoric rise in strength of the body and mind, and similarly, meteoric recovery or acquisition of good health. With it comes the ability to feel responsible and be responsive to life.

It is essential that the practice of yoga and Dhyana continue daily till possible in one's lifetime. You do not need to devote more than an hour to this practice daily, which is essential for every individual who went through the first step of gaining control over their senses.

But the practice of step 2 of yoga and Dhyana are useless without the practice and its perfection achieved in the first step explained—the control over the palate and the subjugation and rejection of sensual pleasures of the mind and body by gaining control over them.

My recommendations to learn and train yourself in yoga and Dhyana, be it India or the world, it is Isha Foundation of Sadhguru Vasudevji. There may be others like Yogananda Paramhansa or the Art of Living by Shri Shri Ravi Shankar, and the same truth I talk about reverberates in other religious teachings like Buddhism, Jainism, Zen, Islam, etc., but my personal choice globally remains the one imparted by Sadhguru Jaggi Vasudevji of Isha foundation for learning yoga and Dhyana.

Well, Sadguru Jaggi Vasudevji is my present and second guru in my life. For some time in my life, I was a disciple of Swami Vivekananda, from whom, reading his inspirational books, I gained him as my guru, in my teenage years, after practising the way and the truth about life shown to me by him. So, Swami Vivekananda is my second guru from whom I gained not only a lot of knowledge of life, but I was firmly saddled in my love for my nation Bharat, reading his books and his teachings.

Action Step 3: From my teachings learnt from my first guru, Swami Vivekananda, as I practise them now, comes another truth about life and how to lead an ideal one. It is the right thing for every human, if he so chooses, to lead a married life and bear children to build his family, to hold his responsibility towards them, and know and experience life to its fullest, but in the right way, as prescribed by my Guru's. Till you marry, you need to follow the life of a Bhramachari, and once you marry, the sex organs are to be put to their rightful intended use only, for procreation— giving birth to your children to raise an ideal family. But once you have given birth to your child or children, you go back to following the path of brahmacharya, a celibate life, which allows you to experience the pleasures of having a family and raising the children, with lots of love and care, and thus leading a successful life of a householder.

It is but obvious that after marriage, if you resort to acquisition of sensual pleasures using the organ for procreation, the same pitfalls of a life full of suffering will definitely happen to you, as you also become incapable of raising your children in the right way, whilst setting a bad example of life to them. You ruin their chances of you being a loving and caring parent to them and become incapable of holding their responsibility, as your wife suffers in the process, with your children.

So, leading an ideal householder's life requires the same discipline again. Well, you can eat normal food as a householder, but overindulgence in food for the gratification of the pleasures of the palate will cause the vital liquid to flow of procreation and be lost, as you suffer in the process. Eating while maintaining a balance in your diet will never cause you any harm, and you can lead an ideal life with your family, observing Bramacharya practice.

Most essentially, sugary foods should be consumed carefully and not overindulged in, Sugar is nothing but white poison, and is also the main cause of cancer! If you avoid sugar, you will be able to lead a life of celibacy very easily, and the vital fluid for procreation, will not leak out, and you will gain the power of Ojas, a spiritual power, which keeps you nearer to God and his perception, besides giving innumerable health benefits and energy and vitality, and alertness of the mind and body. An easy way to balance your food is to consume a good portion of raw salads and fruits daily, as an essential part of your diet, to allow the Bram Acharya practice to continue, in your happy family life. This goes for both the husband and wife.

Well, if you follow the above three steps and lead a life of merit, suffering will never touch you or your family. Nor will you make anybody else suffer in your midst, as you live a life of high karma, full of happiness and blissfulness.

Now coming to the title of the chapter: 'Could Hitler have been like Jesus, if he knew how to be one?' Well, of course, he could have been like Jesus in his karma. I don't mean literally, but he had all the other traits. He was a genius, very capable as a dictator, had all the skills to rise to greatness as the head of a nation, but the only problem he had was he was ignorant of the truth about life, was far from reality, and had absolutely no idea about the nature of our human existence. But suppose he knew this truth, he practised the above three steps in his process of living a life, as a dictator, he would have been kind to everybody, violence and an insurmountable ego would have been very far from him, he would have worked as the most likeable leader in history from whom the milk of human kindness would have flowed towards all like an ocean. His work then would have been akin to a truly great man, whom all would have loved and celebrated as their most beloved leader.

Would he then not be closer to Jesus? The real problem? It lay in his ignorance of the truth of life.

Chapter 4

God Does Not Need Armies of Men to Fight for Him

Here, we address the various conflicts and acts of terror that are taking place in the world, and how we can call an end to them by finding solutions to de-escalate the wars being fought in the name of religion and land acquisition.

Here we will address the war an area of conflict being fought in the name of God and religion. The first among them is Syria. It is the number 1 conflict and war on our Mother Earth today that needs immediate resolution.

Syria: The main ground of all conflicts, in fact, the mother of all conflicts going on in our world is the 7-year conflict of Syria. It is a religious war within the Islamic community and Islamic group of nations, in whom other counties in the world are involved and are fighting a proxy war by taking sides, in whom the superpowers, both the USA and Russia, are aligned on opposite sides, who are fuelling the war and the conflict, with their own group of nations on either side supporting them and joining in the proxy war.

The reason for the war—it is a religious conflict within the two sects of Islam, the Shia versus the Sunni Islamic groups.

Why has the war not ended over these 7 years? It is because the war defies resolution, simply since the two superpowers, the USA and Russia—who can never defeat each other, as they are the nuclear powers and have access to vast resources to use— are part of the proxy war and are fighting against each other, taking opposite sides of the conflict, they make the Syrian war continue. There can be no winner in this war, thus. So, it defies resolution till date! On the one side, it is the Russians, who are supported by Iran and Turkey, who support the military Government of Syria, headed by the Dictator Basher al Assad. And on the other side, it is the USA, whilst demanding an end to the conflict, supporting the rebels of Syria and having nations from Europe and Islamic nations like Saudi Arabia who give moral and funding support to help the rebels capture the land of Syria.

In this mother of wars, who is suffering? It is the people of Syria. They are caught up in a dreadful war, which never seems to end, and the most severe atrocities are being committed on them, month after month, day after day, being the war victims, as the armies fight each other and inflict the most inhuman cruelties, carnages and massacres which are inflicted on them as they are done to death from both the sides in the proxy war.

The Russians do not co-operate as they want their piece of influence over the war, and the world as a superpower, as they have the cold war with the USA, still going on. They are mindful of shielding their sphere of influence and power over as a superpower. So, the USA and the allied nations who are against Russia—even if they wish to call an end to the war and put a stop to the deadly atrocities on humans being committed there—are helpless and unable to do so.

It should not be very difficult to realize that the center point, or the primary source of terrorism, or all the acts of terrorism across the world, the lynchpin is Syria, across the globe, the main motivation for all the terrorist attacks, and all other fronts of religious wars originates presently from Syria, for example, Palestine, Afghanistan, Kashmir in India to a certain extent, etc.

The religious war is of a dastardly nature because chemical weapons are being used on the civilians of Syria. This has happened several times— the children of Syria are prime targets of chemical warfare, so are women and innocent civilians. The situation is so desperate that self-styled liberators of Syria, motivated by this dastardly situation there, where massacres of the innocent of Syria are taking place, which is now in its 7th year, it has become the main source of motivation and the inspiration for all the daring acts of terrorism.

Terrorist attacks are being carried out in different parts of the world and also fuels the enmity on all other fronts of religious wars being fought all over the world. The situation in Syria has become the hotbed of terrorism across our world today. Particularly also because of the fact, that there seems no end to the war being fought in Syria. So, the birth of several terrorist groups, bombing in Europe and the rest of the world goes on unabated, spoiling the name of the followers of Islam in the world today.

So, what do we do about this situation, how do we untangle this situation, stop the spreading violence across the world? Well, the key person who can help end the war is obviously the US president, as the U.S. holds the prime position as a Super power.

Since that time, in the 2020's, the Syrian war has ended, with the Sunni and Shia of Islamic community, called for a Truce to finally close this flashpoint in the World!

Let us now discuss about World Peace, I feel it is definately achievable in our world today!

Starting with a faboulous idea!

Whosoever ever heard of any of the president of America trying to befriend his most dangerous enemy: Russia by engaging in friendship?

Befriending Russia would be the best thing that could happen to the US and the world. If the two superpowers were to align and be strong friends, does it not call for an end to the cold war, the de- escalation of all conflicts in the world, this will also be a call to the de-escalation of the nuclear and conventional arms race going on in the world? Can it not start the new era of nuclear disarmament in the world? Well, if the two biggest adversaries of the world come together in friendship, in mutual cooperation, and work and conduct the affairs of the world with the aim of mutual benefit, will we not witness a new world order, which will start the golden era for all humanity on our Mother earth?

Currently, the world is split up into two parts,where nations have aligned with either sides of superpowers, and that is the reason these other nations oppose each other. But if there is a fusion of friendship between the two groups of nation- states who today fight a cold war, this will end the conflicts in the world by them coming together with a view of the common purpose of mutual benefit, will this world not be a better place to live in? Definitely! Then what is the need for so many nuclear weapons and the disputes and the conflicts going on in our world today, if this were to happen?

If the U.S. President demonstrates, this spirit to end conflicts. Then, there could be lasting peace achieved between USA and Russia, to Completely change the scenario for the better! Just by changing the ways and opening their hearts to love one another, such a grave threat to the world will be eliminated!

It is only the President of U.S. who can bring about such a drastic change and do this. If this can be done, I don't know why for him it should take even a minute longer to achieve the same for the people of our world right away! This would be instrumental in achieving lasting peace by closing all the conflicts in the world!

The only way to stop all the war's being waged there, is for all nations who are involved in the proxy war's come together on a common platform and hold a meeting of the nation states, to put an end to the war's. This is only possible if the US and the Russians come together on a common platform with friendship being established between them. Then surely, all the war's in our world will see an end finally.

So then, who can help the efforts to promote friendship between the US and Russia? It is the U.S. President as a leader who needs to facilitate, and lead the way, towards holding the all- important meeting of the member states, to end the proxy war's in the world, who is capable, who can do it successfully, and who can understand the logic and who enjoys the stature today of a world leader, to lead this mission, and accomplish this for all humanity.

The U.S. President is the one, who is fully capable of advising and leading this effort to not only end the war, but to call an end to terrorism the world over, and to start the process of nuclear disarmament, and to write a new chapter in the annals of human history on our planet.

What a beautiful and wonderful place to live and enjoy this world for all of us it would be!

Indeed, God never needed armies of men to fight for him. He would bless us with happiness, if we gave up this stupid idea on our Mother Earth, for all eternity to come!

What would we gain, if all the conflicts in the world were to stop? Well we are giving our future generations, a bright and sweet future. Do we not want to leave this world to be a better place to live in for our children? We need to bring lasting peace in the world, and since there will be no more conflicts left in the world after the friendship of Russia and the USA are cemented in brotherhood, we can achieve nuclear disarmament, and trash the stock piles of nuclear weapons on our earth. For this the involvement of china, in a friendly relationship with both the super powers is also necessary! As lots of the stock piles are lying in china also!

Actually, the greatest gift from God to humanity and all life on earth is our Mother earth- our nest, where we live and die, as our own. He intended us to enjoy it, and not destroy it by fighting amongst each other. He wanted us to live peacefully and joyfully and in bliss on this Mother earth.

Instead what have we done? We made nuclear weapons to end the world, we defiled the earth with environmental degradation, we continue to suffer by fighting amongst each other, in many conflicts all over the world. All this tension is making us lose focus on the main issues, if everlasting peace is established, we can re-focus on issues such as restoring back the ecological balance on this earth, economic development, employment generation, removing famines in our world, Drinking water shortage. raising the standard of living in poor nations, and focusing of the biggest need of all humanity, to spread and develop human consciousness on this mother earth.

To the more recent developments, we need to make a note on the war in Gaza strip of palestinians and Israel, which defies all limits of cruelty in the Genocide Going on, by the Isralies on the Palestinians, reminds us of Hitler and his ways adopted by Israel. Then there is the war and famine in Sudan, Rohigya refugees, which needs a remedy. A major one is the imperialistic invation of Ukaraine by Russia, war going on since more than 2 years!

I am sure these recent conflicts will be definately, be closed soon, as we hope Mrs. Kamala Harris gets elected for the Presidency of the United States of America, she is Currently the Vice-President of the United States of America, in comingelection's in November 2024!

She is one leader who cares, can feel the pain & suffering of Humanity, and has the will and capability to adress the issues effectively!

Most definitely God does not need armies of men to fight for him, he is angry on us for what we are doing now!

Chapter 5

With Almighty 24 x 7:-
The Elixir of Life Part 2

When you know the technical perspective to life, the knowledge of life is with you, you slowly move to the next stage.

I call the next stage: With almighty 24x7!

Just to recap Part 1. As a first step you detoxify your body, by putting it on a diet for a minimum of 9 months to a year. You ate a combination of raw vegetables including Bitter Gourd + Neem leaves and other vegetables. That is after the puberty stage has come, and you are a bachelor teenager!

This made you gain control over your faculties, and your spiritual intellect blossomed. Then as you started this special diet, you also became a Bramacharya, and were Celibate.

The next step explained was, you learnt the Yoga, Pranayama & Dhayana of Consciousness-for example Inner-engineering program of Sadhguru Jaggi Vasudevji, of Isha foundation, or Art of Living, or any such reputed Indian Institution.

During your Detoxification, you practiced this special Yoga, and lead a Celibate life for a year.

As I explained to you, you will gain control of your Palate, Well-being will come to you, and your Consciousness will broaden immensely to include our world and understand it well.

So, one year is over, and you finished your Special Diet of Detoxification, continuing Daily Yoga and following a Celibate life.

Now comes the finale:- You start your prayers daily, where you bow down to the Almighty, this may be the Kabba for Muslims, or Mataji or any of the deities like Balaji, Ganesha, Krishna, Shiv, etc., Lord Jesus for Christians, Buddha for Buddhists, Waheguru for the Sikh's, Tirthankar for Jains and so on.

In this powerful process, as you practice the same, for months on end, now {You eat regular food} but remain Celibate, do your Spiritual Yoga, and offer prayers to the Almighty God every day.

One day! You will find the Almighty, the invisible one, will connect to you!

You will soon converse with him, and you will listen to his guidance, and you will carry out the tasks of life, as per his instructions.

Now he is living in you. The food you eat he will also enjoy. If you want anything good in life, you ask him what you should do. He will guide you every step of your life.

When you follow his instructions well, you will gain what you want, if it is Meritious.

This is a learning process; you will be with the Almighty 24x7! As you live your life.

You need to understand one or two things in this process, you need to do your prayers to God every day, to stay connected to him.

Second bowing to him is important, you bow to him, by touching your forehead to the ground or floor, minimum 7 to 13 times, while you pray to him. You can bow down from a kneeling position, or by standing up and going all the way down, touching your forehead to the floor, 7 to 13 times minimum when you pray to him. Say loving words to him, say words in his praise, ask for his blessings, ask for his forgiveness, every time you bow down, and stay there to pray to him.

This 7 to 13 times bowing to him to pray, by touching the floor with your head to the ground, should be done minimum 3 times a day. Best to do this once early in the morning, then, once before lunch, and the 3rd time before dinner in the evening. But this does not mean, you discontinue your yoga, Pranayama and Dhayana. This also has to be done every day, with the prayers once at least.

Best to do your Yoga sadhana, before your prayers in the morning, and continue your prayers, once you finish, your yoga sadhana.

All along this way, as time goes by, your perception of the Almighty will keep increasing, and you will be able to stay connected to him, every moment of the day. You will also connect to all those who are similarly doing what you are doing and are similarly endowed with this Superconscious connectivity with the Almighty.

Your health will keep improving, your well-being will happen, with a gain in strength.

You may marry and have a family with your Children, but as explained in Part 1, Sexual activity has only one purpose, that of procreation, once you conceive, you need to go back to your celibate life. While you continue with your prayers to God every day and do your Yoga daily also.

You will be blessed with a happy married and successful life, with the blessings of the Almighty God!

Every good deed you do, God will bless you, and shower his blessings on you. You will realize your goals in life, and be one with God, till the time to depart from this heavenly world comes!

Let me introduce you to the concept of Dua, which is, after you pray to him, you ask for his mercy to bless you to achieve something for you, or your family, or anyone. It may take time, but if your Dua is worthy, beneficial, and Meritos, it will reach God, and you may be blessed by him, and your Dua may come true.

Yoga, Pranayama, Dhayana, Prayers, celibacy, and when needed, Dua every day is mandatory, to stay connected to God and offer your love to him and get his blessings and love from him too!

May God bless you!

Chapter 6

Dire Need to Change of Approach in Education Today: An Amalgamation of the Science of Inner Engineering with External Engineering

Well, essentially, we find a lot of child suicides in the form of education being imparted today to our children. We find failure in exams is something difficult for children to handle apart from the competition which marks our educational system today. While many children drop out of school, and many are misled and led astray into a way of life leading to their ruin, eventually in life. Well, I found lots of highly qualified individuals failing to find a suitable job despite their education. I also found graduates, living by earning their living by driving taxis, many have tried to start a business and have failed, are depressed and frustrated with what they are doing. Some have got to consuming intoxicants and are near ruining their lives. Some have failed society completely and have become part of the anti-social elements of our society. Some have taken to liquor after marriage and children, jeopardising the lives that are dependent on them by their behaviour.

Why is there so much failure in individuals despite being educated? And why many who have not even received basic qualifications, were underprivileged are the stars of our society today? Then I hear about many successful people, who did not even receive basic educational qualifications. Their lives and their achievements are an inspiration to the entire nation, to the society or even the world!

How come the logic becomes reverse sometimes? The highly educated are failures, and those who have almost no access to education are the pride of our world? Then what is the use of such education? What is the use of spending so much time and money and efforts on education by the parents, if they are not even sure or can't even assure themselves that their children will be successful in their lives? What a waste? Why is it sometimes a curse to be part of the privileged part of the society today? One tends to think? Why does logic not work here? What is this form of education today, that turn out batches of failures or lopsided half-successful people being churned out of our schools and universities today on a constant basis? Surely, something is missing in our educational system.

Well, the reason for this is not far to find if you ask those uneducated and underprivileged lots of people, who are not only very successful but are stars of our society, who are great men, the backbone of nations and our society today. Well, these individuals experienced those realities in life and gained the education, albeit by chance, that part of the education, in abundance which was absent in the schools and universities of today. This experience made the conventional education, which they did not receive, irrelevant in terms of importance to their lives. They would tell you, all that they missed not going to the schools and colleges, they picked up this knowledge on their own, in an easy way, since what they experienced was very powerful and was driving their lives right now, which made conventional education irrelevant to them.

The conventional type of education is all about the knowledge of making, building and creating what we witness externally in our world, meaning that which is learnt by applying the intelligence of our brains and minds, including medical science. Our brains function as our tools to understand and manipulate, to our comfort, that which we see and observe, outside our body, and including our body and our minds. These sciences are of physical nature; they are based on engaging our intellect, be it our body or what we see outside our body our materialistic world, or that which engages our minds either psychologically or emotionally. These are all things I wish to qualify as our external world.

We are not even our body or our mind. If we were to close our eyes and sit without even our thoughts in our minds, what is left of us? Nothing! With our eyes closed, even the external environment becomes irrelevant! But we are still alive and conscious, aren't we? That which is still conscious and alive in this state, that is what we really are! We are that nothing, which is still alive and conscious of itself ! When we took birth, we came with nothing of our own, and we know we are all mortal beings; when we die, we take nothing with us, of that we accumulate, including our body and our minds. Our minds and our thoughts, we leave behind. We had a name, well, the name too, we leave behind. Once we depart, our names which were our identity also, we leave behind. We were born in our mothers' womb. Since then, we accumulated, some part of this earth for a temporary period, and when we leave, whatever we accumulated from this earth, including our body, our mind and our name, we leave behind! So, we came from nothingness and went back to nothingness! But we were alive, but we lived our life, and either enjoyed or suffered the world! So obviously, we are not the body or the mind, then what are we? Surely we are something higher than the body or the mind, we generally like to call it our soul, but it is the Great one, or part of it, which created this world, this body and this mind, which lived, because it did!

So, the science that teaches us about ourselves, about our nothingness, and makes us familiar and brings it into our perception, makes us experience this nothingness, that which we essentially are, is the science of our inner self. This inner self is what had the greater intelligence to accumulate a part of the earth, for a temporary period. Well, it created and manufactured our body and our mind to use it as a tool, to exist and live on our Mother Earth.

So, the body and the mind were created by a superior intelligence, which is beyond the body and the mind, which later were used as tools to study our external world and create all this engineering we see outside our body and mind and the physical world that surrounds us! So, what is primary to us, our body, our mind, or this external world that we engineered for our bodily and mental comforts, or is it that inner self, which perceived the world, came from nothingness, and when we shed our body and mind, departs into nothingness? It is the conscious one doing everything in us, for us, but somehow, the way we are generally, if we do not make the effort, we will never have any knowledge of our inner self, remain half conscious, only to feel we are alive, but never realise this truth or know the true nature of our existence and perceive our inner self throughout our life. We will live half consciously, in a lopsided manner and die our natural death, full of misery, and bouts of circumstantial joy which came our way accidentally!

Well, there is a separate science to know the inner self and perceive our true nature! The science of knowing this inner self is called Yoga and Dhayana of consciousness. You may call this as Enlightment! In olden days enlightment was not common, but in our modern world today, enlightment and the science of gaining it is the natural birth right of every human! Well it should be too! Yoga and Dhayana is the Science, through which we perceive the Great one, our Atma and Parmatma (God),and know the truth about our life and the true nature of our existence. This science is the primary science, and that which we create, in the external world surrounding us, is actually created by our mind and body, by us (we are our inner self) using them as our tools, to decipher and engineer that which we see externally around our body and mind, to facilitate our living, and for the comforts of our lives. The whole of our external engineering is to sustain our lives and enjoy the world we are born in!

In our modern education, the focus is only on the tools, our body and our mind, and the engineering of our external world, without the creation of any perception or knowledge of our inner self, which is the primary knowledge, which is not taught in any of our schools and universities of today. And those of us, who luckily bumped into the knowledge of our inner self and felt and perceived it, knew the science of Consciousness and applied it to their lives, are the successful people, who hold the entire world in awe. Many of them may have come from the underprivileged background, never received the secondary education taught in the schools or colleges, but are very successful and happy in their lives, with the consciousness gained through the primary knowledge og the Inner Self. For such people, acquiring the knowledge taught in the schools and colleges are a matter of pittance, they can acquire this knowledge, just by their observation or by self-study, which is a very rapid process, in comparison to the time it takes to learn in our schools and colleges, by our children, who are not aware of the true nature of our existence, and are only, half conscious to their lives.

Many of the children studying in schools and colleges may also be lucky to acquire the perception of the inner self and be well rooted in the knowledge of the inner self. Thus, they may be fully conscious and aware of the truth about their lives, and they turn out to be very successful in their lives, just as the ones who are shining out in our society today, coming from a more ordinary background in terms of material wealth. But generally, these children may gain knowledge of Science of consciousness a bit later in life, than those children, who do not have the material privileges of life but start off with the primary knowledge and experience of life, very early in their lives, so their Greater achievements in life!

So, what do we do about the world today, having many people as failures in their lives, due to not being conscious, and not having the experience of the primary truth about life? And lost in the Secondary knowledge? Obviously, we need to amalgamate, the two types of education which are necessary to be 100% successful in our world, we need to teach both the primary knowledge and make the children in our school experience and perceive their inner self, which is of a static nature (remains same as time moves forward in our existence), but essential at the right age, when their bodies and minds become receptive to such knowledge and experience, but also teach them the secondary knowledge of life: the knowledge of the external world around us, and how to manipulate it, to enjoy it and use it for our purpose in our lives, enriching our lives further, which is of an evolutionary nature, and changes with us as time moves forward in our existence.

We cannot de-value the fact that among the underprivileged population of children, many children are doubly unlucky, they do not get access to or ever experience, either the primary knowledge of the inner self or the secondary education of the external sciences. So, education both primary and secondary needs to be made compulsory for all children, regardless of their background and status of their lives in our society materialistically, the government needs to sponsor both the amalgamation of the primary sciences and the secondary sciences external in nature, and make the education free, impartial and compulsory for all. And as we amalgamate both the science of the primary inner self, with the secondary science of the external engineering, then, mostly, the failures and the aberrations we see in the lives of our children, soon to turn into adults will be mostly eliminated. Everybody going to school will be nearly 100% successful in their lives. No suicides, no failures for anybody generally! This is the need of the modern era! Technology and Enlightment together in our lifes!

Our World will then receive a big dose of fast forward with success and joy coming to all! This should be our new mantra for education for our children!

So, what needs to be taught to the children today is to make them aware and perceive the truth about life, which will make them not only successful but feel responsible for their life and responsive to the world around them.

Well, the solution is much the same, as detailed in my earlier chapter, educate them on how to gain control over their palate, and the practice of Bhramcharya, once they cross the age of puberty, and secondly, to teach them the science of inner self, or for that matter the practice of the right type of yoga, to gain the knowledge and perception of the Great one or Parmatma, as their own very true nature.

Well, let them know the truth, which is crucial to their life-the correct use and purpose of the sex organ was meant to be used for by the creator, for procreation, and make them aware of the failure in life they will face, and the pitfall of causing ruin to their lives, by misusing the sex organ to experience sensory pleasures in life, and if they do not know and follow the steps necessary to establish their life.

This type of school is the ideal one as, at a young age, the children come to know of the truth, and they get a right start to their lives. This primary knowledge, the science of yoga & Dhayana will make them fully conscious, healthy, and capable to realise the responsibility they carry towards the society and the world, at large, being born as a human. And, at the same young age, they are successful in acquiring the external sciences, in the form of external engineering. That is, they will be certainly successful in learning what the conventional education teaches them today, to manipulate the external environment scientifically to make better use of the Mother Earth's resources for their benefit, for enriching the living experience further with responsibility. When they pass out of college, they are fully equipped to deal with the world, as they enter the formal society, being responsible citizens of not only their nation but as global citizens, well, with no fear or chance of their failure in life for them or their parents or our Society.

In ancient India, the focus was entirely on the science of the inner self, whilst erroneously, the nurturing, and development of the external sciences were ignored or overlooked, so those civilisations, which did give high importance to the external sciences, that is the manipulation of the external world, they invaded our Bharat, and ruled over us and exploited us, especially the British, for over 250 years!

So, it is obvious, the external engineering sciences are equally important for survival. Our ancients ignored it to our peril! Now in the modern world, we are overlooking the sciences of the inner self, with chances of even greater consequences, the failure of the entire educational system, and society itself ! Apart from the degradation of the environment, which is being led again, due to the same malady that plagues our Society today, and as a consequence, the wrongful exploitation of the environment, is being done, in a unsustainable, and irresponsible manner, creating harm to our Mother Earth, to such an extent that our own human species are facing a threat from the damage done to the ecological system of our planet by us out of our Ignorance. And following the sciences of external engineering, without the wisdom or knowledge of the inner self.

So now the desperate need of the hour is to amalgamate both the external and internal sciences, to turn out educated individuals, who know the truth fully, they run their lives successfully, but with responsible behaviour towards the use of the environment, and help restore the ecological balance of our planet.

Bharat was exploited due to lack of attention given to the external sciences and was enslaved. Now today, we almost completely have forgotten the ancient sciences of the past, and having becoming to a great extent, slaves to the western way of living, who do not fully understand the science of the inner self, are now focusing only on the external sciences in education all over the world, calling for the ruin of not only the individuals, but society, and also in the process causing irreparable damage by the constant exploitation and misuse of our Mother Earth's resources.

Sadly, this is what ails our society today, individuals formally joining the formal society without any sense of responsibility they need to carry, being human. So, many individuals are turning out failures, leading the society in the same direction, and the same way, then nations and finally, the world is turning chaotic and is disrupted with this type of system being followed today.

I would like to mention a special note about our country India. We follow the same books in schools, which are the same, the western world, or conventional education, the west is following. Are we not aware, that we as Bharat, have been the farmland of great men, both leaders, and the holy sages of our past, that no other country can equal in the whole world? Bharat is the hot bed of Spirituality and the Ancient wisdom and Science of Conciousness!

We also ignore to teach Sanskrit, which is the mother of all languages, and the pride of our nation and learning it, all of us can read and understand the ancient texts, written thousands of years back, in its originality, which explains everything very clearly and teaches us the sciences of the inner self which is the ancient wisdom of our ancient culture, written by our ancient and sacred sages of our past. This language disconnect with the past is the real reason for the growing disorientation, and chaos we see today progressing forward alarmingly under the western cultural influence of our Indian society, and our nation.

If Sanskrit was made the compulsory language in our schools, the problem will end quickly! Why is Ramayana, the Mahabharata, the Vedas, the Upanishads, the Puranas, Patanjali Yoga Sutras, Agama Shastras, our ancient martial arts of Kalari, and our entire, folklore, the rich culture and heritage of our Bharat, not taught in our schools? It should be!

Essentially, the call and need now, for the future of our Educational System, and the solution to our problems which have reached a critical stage in our society today, is to teach both the science to know and experience the inner self, and also learn and be taught and to be aware and conscious about the true nature of our existence, and the science of external engineering, which we already have in our conventional education we teach today! Both amalgamated and taught will lead to the Success of our Society and our world today! God bless!

Chapter 7

Ending the Suffering of the Poorest of the Poor in Our Bharat!

Namaste!

I wish to draw your attention to the people in our Bharat, who are at present suffering the most and the pain they are undergoing in their life, is unbearable. If we were to imagine ourselves in their place, we can feel the misery and pain that they are going through. Yes, you guessed it right-I am talking about the poorest of the poor citizens amongst us- the beggars of Bharat!

Coming to the point directly, in the form of my suggestion as a responsible citizen of India, I wish to point out that from the nation's budget you have allocated a total of 10 Billion Dollars to spend on the Bullet train, to be built between Mumbai and Ahmedabad, and there are other lacks of crores of such expenditure you have earmarked for various projects and schemes from the Government of India.

Has it occurred to you that, before you allocated this tax payers money on projects, that such allocation you have done, you should have thought first of the poorest and the most suffering in India? At stake here is human life-that should get the first attention, are they any less citizens of our Bharat compared to us?

Is it not, that they are not in a condition to help themselves, that they continue to suffer? They are more visible to you in the cities, they come to your door to beg-you see them crying out of pain, and hear their lamenting to beg you to help them, and still hardly any help is given to them.

India lacks nothing today, it is self-sufficient, it can help itself like other countries in the world. So, for Bharat, the first task is for you to come to the rescue of these unfortunate citizens of India. I draw your attention to other nation's where no such citizen is suffering in this manner-U.K. Saudi Arabia, Japan, Singapore etc. where there is no such Citizen of those countries that are so desperate and left uncared for by their Government.

Dear Pradhan Mantriji, it is your duty and duty of your Government to respond adequately to such poor in India. We Individual citizens can help only a few of them, with our limited resources, and that to not as a continuous responsibility.

Among our such poor are children, women, the disabled, and the very old. I suggest you start accounting for them, the children should be packed off in homes, and provided education and other facilities. Among the rest you need to identify those who can work, and we teach them some skill to sustain themselves, including the women. And the badly disabled and the too old, need to be rehabilitated in special care homes. They need to be provided chappals, clothes, food, water, medicines for any ailments that need to be treated, at Government expenditure.

Are you aware presently, what is their condition? They eat and drink from the garbage leftovers, they have nobody to care for them. No love and caring, no family. They are moving barefoot, either half or fully naked on the streets, be it rain, summer or winter, they bear the weather conditions, the insects and wild animals they are exposed to, are apart from the pollution. In fact, when they fall prey to these, their dead bodies have to wait on the street, till the municipal cleaners, pick them up and dump their bodies in the dump yard, they do not get even a decent burial!

How can we continue to allow this? Bharat is our Sacred land, it is our Janmabhoomi, where Raja Ram once graced this land. Is this our Ram Rajya? In this sacred land countless Saints and Great men have lived and taken birth, does our Bharat Mata deserve this, do the citizens of Bharat deserve this predicament? We need to act fast and sensibly on this subject, by allocating adequate money from our exchequer to take care of these most unfortunate amongst us without any delay and on a war footing!

In this regard I wish to draw your attention to the data in your Niti Ayog, the Tendulkar committee method, (2016) which made a study of our poor: There are a total of nearly 27 crore people who live below the poverty line (BPL), of them 6 crores reside in the urban cities and 21 crores in the rural areas, and their percapita monthly spending is less than 1,000 rupees, that is exactly what they would be able to collect by begging in a month!

So Dear Pradhan Mantriji, my humble request to you is to rescue these poor, and be blessed by Bharat Mata forever!

Bharat Mata ki Jai! Jai Shri Ram! May God bless the poor of Bharat!

Pranam!

Chapter 8

Status of Our Government Schools

Problem Area 1: Status of our Government Schools: It is no secret that the government schools and colleges exist in a pathetic condition and that no lower and middle-class citizens of India will choose them as a credible option to educate their children. It is the very poor families who cannot afford education for their children, who admit their children in government schools. For most of the population, private schools are the only credible option for their children. Moreover, key statistics about the school infrastructure in our nation puts a question mark on the availability of credible infrastructure and resources for education in our nation. A very poor state of affairs indeed!

Given below are the extracts on school infrastructure and facilities available in our nation taken from the government website of Nitiayog. Some points to note particularly in this data is that 75% of all primary schools in India are government schools, and only 25% come from the private sector. Secondly, of these government schools that exist in our country, 85% are schools located in rural areas, and only 15% of the government schools are in urban areas. Further, 70% of Government secondary schools are situated in rural areas, and only 30% of Secondary schools are in urban areas.

Here is the data in actual numbers:

Education-related

1. For Primary education:

   Total schools in India as per data updated 2015–16: 14,05,027.

   Of this, government schools are 10,43,151, accounting for 74.2% of total schools. Of these, the rural government account for 85.1%

   Of this, the private school count is 3,24,263 accounting for 23.1% of total schools, and of these, the rural private account for the balance.

   The balance Madrasas or unrecognised is 2.7%.

2. Secondary education related: Total school count is 2,52,176,

   Of these, the rural account for 1,75,176 and urban account for 77,024.

It should not surprise you that the government schools' teachers' salary or total renumeration, anywhere across our nation, is much higher than the teachers teaching in the TOP and best private schools across the country. But still the best talent in teachers are absorbed and take up jobs in private schools only, despite low pay scales. But if the pay is significantly higher in Government schools, why do the best teachers flock to private schools and shun the government schools as a possible alternative?

This statistics and facts are exactly the core of the problem in our educational system. Most of the government schools lack the basic credible infrastructure to promote the cause of education. There are many government schools lacking proper classrooms; they lack proper toilet facilities, both for male and female students and teachers.

There is inadequacy or absence of other facilities such as school transport, computer labs, science labs, facilities for sports and yoga and, further, for extracurricular, activities like teaching facilities for drawing, painting, music, school library, singing and dancing, martial arts, etc. Moreover, reasonable facilities for the upkeep of the school premises, regarding sanitation and cleaning are absent. When we visit a government school, we get a sinking feeling that this is not what our children deserve! Lots of schemes of midday meals by the government have been launched in government schools. However, most of the food served is unhygienic and unpalatable. Milk as a beverage in all schools should be a must for the children, but most of the government schools don't serve palatable quality milk in the schools.

There are no proper uniforms, books, bags, shoes, etc., made available of any reasonable quality to the students enrolled in the government schools.

With such poor infrastructure, facilities and services offered in government schools, the fact that none of the talented teachers will ever seek a job in government schools is not surprising, even if the pay offered is higher.

With no proper administration and monitoring in our government schools, the dropout rate of students enrolled are very high. So are the results generated in government schools in board examinations.

So, what do we do about this? The first duty of the Government of India is to invest massively on government school infrastructure and facilities and teacher training, and teacher schools.

It is also obvious that the existing teachers staff available in our nation, is highly inadequate, and so is the number of government schools available, to meet the demands of the population of students which is again growing with the growth of our country's population.

If you were to check, the teacher-student ratios, available in India and compare it such data in the develop economies, the ratio of teachers available per student is appalling and hugely inadequate. There are approximately 6 million teachers in India, and the current population of students in India are above 315 million, which means the teacher to student ratio in India is 53 students per teacher. And this is just a statistic; the deployment of teachers in schools is a question mark.

According to one report, which demonstrates the anomalies existing in our educational system, above 1 lakh schools in India, in the government sector, have only one teacher assigned to each of these schools! So, there is only a single teacher per school, which again raises a question mark on the educational facilities in our nation.

In developed nations such as Japan, UK, etc. the student to teacher ratio is 16 to 18 students per teacher!

If you were also to check the number of schools to population ratios, available within our nation, again the glaring inadequacy stands out. Cross checking our government school ratio to population with other developed economies again brings to light the enormous inadequacy of the number of schools available to meet the demands of our student population currently.

How can a nation progress, when its main pillar of strength, educational facilities, available are so poor! What pace of economic development can we realistically expect with most of the population uneducated or inadequately educationally facilitated?

The key to developed nations wealth and wellbeing are the educational facilities created by the government for its citizens. Education is compulsory and free in most of the developed economies of the world. Adequacy and availability of adequate educational facilities is the secret to the sustained economic progress of all developed nations in the world.

Also,in the developed economies,the ratio of government schools is even more skewed.Most of the schools in developed economies are government schools, and the count of private schools is negligible in developed nations. Education as a working institution of those developed nations occupy the pride of place, among Government run Institutions, and are a basic and most vital institution functioning, to serve their nations interest and are the fulcrum points driving their economies forward and are the main pillars of strength of these nations.

With quality education available, quality jobs, business, innovation, jobs for the young and aspirant population will be created, this is the secret mantra of success of any nation.

So my request to the Government of India is to give a major part of the budget allocation to make the existing government schools of the best quality, with quality infrastructure and facilities, and so the teaching staff training and teacher training institutes to train our existing teachers, and to encourage the teaching as a profession in our nation by creating attractive conditions for this noble profession. Major investment in starting and establishing government schools in large numbers, enough to meet the demands of our nation's growing student population.

Education should be the major area for government investment out of the budget and resources allocation and become a major centre of expending the energies of all government resources and attention for the next decade to make our nation equal in economic development to developed economies.

Chapter 9

Jai Javan Jai Kisan!

The most vital and crucial the part of our nation Jai jawan! Well, we need to realise that the security and peaceful atmosphere we enjoy today, is mainly due to the Sacrifices our nation's Jawans or the army has made by laying down their lives in service of our nation. We all civilians can enjoy our lives only because of them. If it is not for them, we can never achieve anything meaningful, as a nation in this world.

But the way we treat our Jawan's, or army, we need to ensure that for every soldier who lays down his life for our country, every member of his family, is lent support by the government of India. They need to be compensated with a heavy sum of money to secure their financial resources, they must compulsorily be provided with a handsome pension, education for his children, and employment opportunities for any earning member of his family, including his spouse, for the rest of their lives.

For all soldiers returning from service from the armed forces, not only should they get a handsome pension for their life, but also a good opportunity to work as a civilian, with a good pay, and this should be their first right! Provided by the government of our country!

So, it is imperative and our duty to take good care of every Jawan, Jai Jawan!

We know for sure that it is the farmers of our nation, and the armed forces in our nation, who are the worthiest citizens of our nation. Through relentless hard work and dedication, our farmers toil the soil to make it give the life nourishing food, be it grains or vegetables or fruits. If they are not able to do their duty, the whole nation suffers, including our economy. Although 75% of our population resides in the rural areas-in the villages, and the contribution to the GDP of the nation from the agricultural and allied industries are only 17.32%. The rest of the GDP comes from the industrial sector at 24.2% and the rest of the GDP comes mainly from the services sector at 57.9%.

So, this proportion is very unhealthy, as in developed countries the contribution of agriculture and allied industries as part of the GDP is below 1% and the part of the population engaged in the agricultural sector is also below 1%. Also, in developed countries, the lion's share of about 70 to 80% of the population is engaged in the services sector and the balance of 19% is engaged for employment in the industrial or manufacturing sector.

This is the real reason, also for the high level of poverty in India. While 75% of Indian population contribute to only 17.2% of GDP. The rest, both the industrial and services sector, contribute to the major part of our GDP, where only 25% of the population is engaged in this sector.

This is the reason for the poor situation the farmers find themselves in, and if rains are deficient, or the crop fails due to any reason, a large part of the Indian population undergoes immense suffering, to the extent that, this becomes the primary cause of farmer suicides in our nation.

Such is the condition of our farmers in our nation. A lot of things need to be done to correct this anomaly in our nation, first quality education needs to be provided in rural areas to enhance the skills of people living in the villages. Secondly, large-scale investment of project fund allocations needs to be invested in the rural sector, we need to develop our villages and raise its standards of development. We continuously focus on developing our major cities, 75% of our focus needs to shift to developing villages. We need not only, good schools and colleges there, proper roads connectivity, hospitals there, electrification density, the government claims that all the villages are electrified, are all the households too? The gas connections are claimed as an achievement, but what % of households has gas connections in the villages? The lack of investment in creation of homes for all citizens living in the villages, continues to be a serious problem, what is the penetration in the villages for all means of communication media, remains a question mark. What about proper drainage connections and sanitation facilities at village level? What about availability of clean drinking water for all who live in our villages? Most significantly, are irrigation facilities available, for all the farmers and villages in India? More significantly, what about development of business and encouragement for starting business for all the entrepreneurs in the villages? What about development of customer friendly banking facilities in the villages. What is the state of rule of law and order in the villages? What part of the village population is educated to take the business sector forward or implement government initiatives?

These are all big question marks, and unless a large part of government initiatives is aimed towards developing the villages, no real progress is possible! We need to try to correct the anomaly we suffer as a nation, mainly focused on agriculture as source of income to re-focus on the industrialisation and development of the services sector as we witness in the developed economies. This statistics of populations engagement in the Manufacturing and services sector, is also the reason, most of the developed nations of the world, like the UK, USA, Europe, Japan, Saudi, etc, are very wealthy nations and carry so much clout in the economic sphere, we need to modernize and develop our nation, so that the contribution of the Manufacturing and services sector, accounts for more than 98% of our GDP, with this we will see the major portion of our population, now in the rural areas well developed, and their productivity enhanced to meet such Standards, and this is only possible by educating and skilling the entire population engaged in agriculture today, to maintain involvement in the sector only to the extent necessary, and the rest encouraged to work in more productive services and manufacturing sectors of our economy, this will surely lead to rapid economic development, and wealth in our nation. Also going as long way in minimising the inequality of wealth distribution in our population. 3 initiatives towards realizing this is abolishing GST on farm produce, second, mandatory crop insurance, loan waivers as and when warranted, and MSP roll out for farmers benefit every crop season. Apart from this schools & hospital & road, rail, even air if feasible for transport development, others, electricity, irrigation, housing and Gas connection, A Class facilities to be developed for the farmers, for their deveopment and well being, raising their standard of living permanently.

Jai Kisan!

Chapter 10

What Are Medicines, What Is Illness and Doctors?

What is illness? Both mental and physical? Why do they occur to us? Can they be cured? It is said that nearly 80% of all illness is self-created, self-inflected, and 15% are created by the unhealthy environment we surround ourselves with, this is created by the way the natural resources are exploited and spoilt by disturbing the natural ecological balance on our Mother earth, by causing destruction of nature by polluting it, gifted by God to us. And only 5% of the diseases are real to the nature of our existence, where the natural process of ageing comes, and some form of diseases come as we get old, to remain as causes for us to depart from this world, as the energy of the body wains as we grow naturally old, and the laws of nature take over our body, and we shed that body, which we accumulated from the earth, from the time we were born. That is, return it back from where we took it in the first place.

Then what is the cause of illnesses of increasing complexity that ail us humans? The diseases come to us, as a consequence of both the physical and mental misbalance we create for ourselves in four ways- Firstly, it is the current lifestyle we adopt, the type of food we eat, and the way we use our body, with a sedentary life style established mostly by all, in our modern society, secondly, the way we use our natural resources, exploiting them in such a way, that we pollute the very environment in which we live, with this environment of pollution taking its toll on us, by inflicting diseases on all humanity. Thirdly, the way we do our karma, in our lives, we shout, we have anger, we show cruelty to others, we exploit other humans who are weaker than us, we behave selfishly, we become self-centred and do not care for others, we hurt other humans, be it family, relatives, or friends, including innocent animals, who are shown the utmost cruelty. Leading a dis-balanced and meritless life and existence, takes a heavy toll on our health.

When we do all this, the creator or a part of him, which is the real life in us, does not feel like staying in the body, such unholy karma, done with our body and mind. So automatically, the creator in us responds, with all types of illnesses, to help it exit a body, by relinquishing its very existence, by causing all sorts of diseases to us. With this type of karma, and living the creator feels, your very existence in the world created by him, is a burden, you do not need to stay on our Mother earth any more, you have become a liability to the process of life itself, in our existence, so an early exit from the world is already on cards with the diseases you get from within you, created by the creator himself now working against you.

But the creator always, gives you chances to amend your life, till you are alive, whilst doing all the bad karma, suddenly, you turn the tide, you start doing good karma, start helping others in need, start loving other humans and animals, you banish anger, and all behaviour which hurt others, instead you become kind, and caring towards others, you shed all bad karma, by living a life of high merit, if people feel your need to exist, you get back love in return for your good karma, then, ultimately the creator feels like continuing to exist in your body, and from being a burden to our Mother earth, you become an asset, if the world needs you, then, the creator, starts curing the diseases he inflicted on your body and mind, you turn healthy, slowly, your time to live on our Mother earth gets extended automatically, as a consequence of your Good Karma, you have a long and lovely, joyful, and happy life to live before you, as deemed by the creator within you, as per your karma.

Medicines are no longer necessary, which are only outside help, or support you have created for yourself, to make you live a life of misery, and in pain of taking all sorts of medicines, to help you rid of your diseases, whilst your karma, continues to be bad, and you are in a downward spiral in your life. How were these medicines created first? They were created by using the intellect of the human mind, to support life, artificially, whilst you do bad karma, and you develop diseases, and you still want to live, maybe miserably and in pain, as you try to fight your diseases, to stay alive, which is not supported by the creator within you which is the real you.

Medicines do not work much, as you continue with your illnesses, against the will of the creator in you, as you continue your bad karma. With bad karma continuing, your consumption of medicines, to help support your life, on our Mother earth goes on increasing. The more bad karma you continue to do in your life, the number, the strength, of medicines, and then ultimately your last resort, of medical intervention, through surgery starts, whilst you experience more and more pain as you are miserable, as you continue to live, with pain in you.

With bad karma, you start living a painful life indeed, with both heavy doses of medicines, and surgeries you invite, through the doctors help, you invoke, at the hospitals with the money you spend of yours in bulk, in your mistaken belief, that you are re-covering, but actually you are going through a process of pain added, by the creator as a punishment for your bad karma.

It remains a fact that, with bad karma continuing, your fate of pain filled life, heading towards your death, continues, this is a decision taken by the creator himself, within you, as he seals your fate, and your limited time on our Mother earth. In this type of life, do you think anybody on this planet, really needs you, or your absence will ever be felt, logically, haven't you become a burden, and a liability for our Mother earth, to continue to allow your existence in it?

Occasionally, you may be greeted by your doctor, that due to the medicines prescribed by him, and administered by you on your body, you are cured! Or the hospital surgeon may declare you safe, as he has been successful in curing your disease! That's a great feeling no? But through the medicines administered, your symptoms have receded, or through the surgical procedure, again the same has happened, you feel happy about it, despite the pain you went through, to achieve it. Or in fact the current ailment under question may in fact have been cured by your doctors! But as your debit of bad karma, continues, new problems take birth in your body, a weakened body, again gets sick after a short duration of mental relief ! And the cycle of diseases and misery continues, unabated, after a brief halt, as the creator ultimately, is the only decision maker of your destiny, and as your bad karma continues, he makes decisions against you, nobody needs you, and the cycle of medicines and surgery continue, whilst you go through more pain, and ultimately you come to your death.

So ultimately, to conclude, the medicines and medical procedures you go through, happen therefore and are the sum of all the bad karma you did, or good karma you abstained from. This is the law of karma, you can feel the joy and happiness of your life, directly proportionate to the balance in good or bad karma you did at any stage of life, none more, none less?

What is then a doctor? Well, the doctor is a qualified scientist, using external engineering, the conventional sciences taught at universities, and hospitals, training institutes, he is a medical scientist, to help cure your body, of all ailments, which you yourself have created for yourself, with the karma you do. It is common knowledge, pious people, who are kind, for whom there is a need from others, and he remains as an asset to society, well really do not need doctors, and diseases are not close to them, and mostly they are very healthy and joyful, happy people, of this earth! Well, those who need doctors utilise their services, by paying their fees, to help themselves by using the expertise of the doctors to cure them of those diseases which they have created for themselves! Well, it's considered a profession of high merit in our society, as they seem to enjoy a noble status in our society, as they are only ones to help you, to save you, from the ire of the creator himself, but of course the relief they provide, is of a temporary nature, if you continue your bad karma. Doctors are costly too, as the science they have knowledge of, they have paid a heavy price both in money, time and efforts to acquire! So, they are very respectable humans, as they ultimately lead you on the path you have chosen, albeit with pain inflicted on your body and mind, to your death ultimately. How well their curing works depends on the type of karma you have done, not by their abilities alone!

Which is the bigger doctor? The human you see before you qualified as a doctor and uses his knowledge and talent to cure you, based on his intellect and body? Or the real doctor of all doctors, the great creator himself, who is the real you, whilst you are unable to perceive him in you today, who decides your destiny, according to your karma, who actually cures you or makes you ill according to the karma you do?

So, these are your illnesses, medicines or doctors, that's exactly what they are in reality!

How to regain your health? The first step is to do good karma, and if it difficult in your present state of affairs, you cannot help yourself, you need help, you are a slave of your senses, and are not aware, of the truth, the true nature of our existence, you need to start anew, as I trust you seem to be going nowhere in your life, you first take a break, and work towards creating this ability in you to do good karma, for this you first need to gain control over your palate, and through it, your sense organs, second step, realise, what the organ for procreation was created by the creator within you was meant for, and become first a Bramahachari, in a married life, if you are married already, or if a bachelor, still the truth remains the same, and then, as a third step learn yoga, or the science of the inner self, what one of my Gurus (Sadhguru) calls inner engineering, and practice it, both in your life, being a Bramhachari, and practising yoga, daily, most of your ailments will get naturally cured, as the creator starts working for you, as with these 3 steps automatically, you turn into an asset for our world, and automatically your Good Karma account starts for you with a bang! If some ailments have advanced, they may require support still from your doctor, till you achieve the balance of good health in your life.

Sometimes, if the ailment is of a critical nature, and it has advanced to a level it cannot be cured, even by a doctor, then, by the three processes, being followed by you, and the Good Karma you start doing, being made possible to you, your life span will definitely go up, you may endure less pain, whilst you continue having the critical illness, you will still have a reasonable quality of life, and life span, unexplainable by your doctors, a wonderful surprise in medical field! Some people have lived with cancer or other such ailments, till their old age, due to their good karma!

From all this one thing is for sure, that Human doctors of today, can never be compared to the supreme doctor who resides in us all, the creator himself, whatever knowledge a doctor uses and can achieve does not and cannot work on you, if you are ill, and if the will of the creator within you is absent, to effect a cure on you, by the entire medical fraternity, no matter how much efforts the doctors put in, no real cures can come, if the creator in you does not will it! And the only way to get cured of diseases, is to secure the will of the creator in you, which will come only with Good Karma, and if you are not aware and conscious, only by making your body and mind capable of Good Karma, through the 3 step process of gaining control over your palate, and sensory organs, by using the organ of procreation for the purpose it was meant for and created only, and by practising yoga, to raise your level of consciousness and awareness, is the only way to start your account of Good Karma leading you to health, wealth, prosperity, happiness, joy, and a blessed and blissful life. This is possible, as the absolute truth, with a curing that comes with preventive measures against all illnesses that which ever could ail you.

You can exit the body, then painlessly, as you grow old, and die of old age, with the sweetest exit possible, before you know it, without much pain in the process, whilst being active till the very end, you leave painlessly, as the creator in you, planned for you!

Chapter 11

The Poor State of Our Government Hospitals

Well, nobody needs an introduction to the poor State of our Government Hospitals. Government hospitals are supposed to offer free services to the citizens of our nation India. But such are they services offered there, or the patient feels, he is entering a hospital, which is going to increase his suffering, with almost no tangible benefit to his health? Well, the poor with more critical illnesses, surely feel, that when they are admitted to government hospitals, if he is lucky, he may come out alive, if he is not, surely, he may not survive and meet his end!

Well, do my words not have a ring of truth around them? For the poor who any way cannot afford any medical treatment, for them the only choice available is more suffering or death in government hospitals?

The government hospitals are kept firstly so unhygienic, that the patient will fall sick in such surroundings. Lots of possibilities of infectious diseases are possible, to a patient admitted to a government hospital. Well, the beds are dirty, have insects, and smell and are very uncomfortable to sleep in. The bathrooms, or restrooms, are very dirty and smelly, they are not cleaned well, and so appear like very dirty public toilets, a further source of infections for the hospitals.

Medicines are available, but you need to grease the hands of hospital authorities to gain access to medicines prescribed by the doctors. Even though the hospital staff is well paid by the government, they are corrupt, and constantly, the poor patient must face the fact that, without greasing the hands of the staff, he cannot get anything done.

The diagnostic equipment, and operation theatres, the critical care wards are again, not only very dirty, and ill maintained, but many do not work, but nevertheless they are used by the hospital.

The doctors are a demotivated lot, who must function in these horrible conditions; they are under government pay, which compared to private hospitals are very poor. They are not motivated to perform well. And many of them are corrupt like the hospital staff.

In no way can a patient feel assured, after entering a government hospital, that he can expect that reasonable care to cure his diseases will be taken by the hospital authorities. In fact, he feels, he will suffer more, as proper care will not come, from the discourteous staff, but the poor man has no option, since he cannot afford the hospital fees of private hospitals, and he thus puts himself under the mercy of government hospitals, as an option of last resort.

Just over a month ago, 18 new born babies died within a span of 24 hours in a well-known public hospital in Ahmedabad. Over 160 children died in a Gorakhpur government hospital in August 2017; 55 children were reported dead in a Nasik government hospital. Number of such deaths and cases of medical neglect are registered each day in government medical centres and hospitals across the country. A few days ago, news reports from the national capital region said that one of the leading hospitals in the region had charged a family a total of INR 18 lakhs for the fortnight-long treatment of a 7-year-old dengue patient. The little girl later died of the disease and the aggrieved parents vented their anger on the Social Media. And this is not an isolated case.

To, add apathy to the whole thing, and you have bodies of the dead being mutilated by dogs in hospital morgues, people carrying home their dead children because the hospital refused them a hearse, Outrages both in the media and on Social Media have become common but the need of the hour is awareness and action.

This is about government hospitals but let us view the statistics of all hospitals in our nation. The total number of hospitals in India is 35,000; having 14 lakh beds. And among them only 2% of all qualified doctors work in rural areas, whereas nearly 70% of the population of India resides in rural areas. According to one survey there is only 1 bed for every 879 people in India. Our government spends less than 1% of the GDP on health care.

India's public healthcare system is also a disaster due to the low funding received by public medical institutions. In fact, comparison to the newly industrialised nations and even among the BRICS countries, India's per capita spends on health care are dismal. India's annual per capita spends on healthcare is pegged at about USD 75, per individual. Compare this with the per capital expenditure of China (USD 420), that of South Africa (USD 570), Russia (USD 893), and Brazil (USD 947) and the difference is a very stark one. The per capita healthcare expenditure in the UK is USD 4003, in Japan is USD 4150, and in the US is USD 9451.

If these figures are not quite enough to reveal the sad state of healthcare in the country, let us see what the government spends. In India, private healthcare services cost about 800 percent the expenditure a patient is likely to incur in a public hospital or medical centre. Despite this, people across rural and urban sectors prefer to seek out private practitioners and medical services. Private spending on health care is about 70 percent of the total expenditure and the government has nearly frozen its healthcare spending. As a nation, we are very far from social security and state-sponsored medical aid, but the mounting charges makes quality healthcare unaffordable for most Indians.

In India there is one government allopathic doctor for every 10,189 and one state -run hospital for every 90,343 people. India has a little over 1 Million allopathic doctors to treat a population of nearly 1.5 Billion people. Of these doctors only 10% work in the state-run hospitals. The shortage of health providers and infrastructure is the most acute in rural areas, where catastrophic health expenses push population of nearly 7 crores into poverty each year. Over 72% of the rural and 79% of the urban population rely on private hospitals for treatment, says a recent survey conducted by the National Sample Survey Office (NSSO). The survey also showed a clear preference for allopathic treatment (90%) over AYUSH (Ayurveda, Yoga, Umami, Siddha and Homoeopathy) in both rural and urban areas. Since both rural and urban sets depended on private hospitals for treatment, their spending for hospitalisation was also higher. The average cost of treatment in a private hospital was Rs. 25,850 as compared to Rs. 6,120 charged in a public hospital.

"The minimum budget for public health should be at least 3–5% of the GDP and we are not even close to that. Incidentally, 86% of rural and 82% of urban population is not covered under any scheme of health expenditure support. To pay for treatment, rural households primarily depended on their 'household income/savings' (68%) and on borrowings Rajesh D Sanghvi (25%) whereas urban households relied much more on their 'income/saving' (75%) for financing expenditure on hospitalisation, than on borrowings (only 18%). Only 12% of urban and 13% of the rural population is under health protection coverage through Rastriya Swasthya Bima Yojana (RSBY) or similar government schemes.

Approximately 22% of Indians are already living below poverty line and if their savings are being used to pay for health then this could indicate one of the contributing factors to their poverty.

This shows the deplorable and sorry state of affairs going on over government hospitals. For the middle class it is well neigh impossible to cover their expenses for medical treatment, and for the Blow poverty line population, 22% of population, estimated which is huge, the government hospitals are the only option. And what lies in store for them, I have just illustrated, the sorry state of government run hospitals.

So, what should be the top priority of the of our government? Spending on government hospitals, and creation of an administrative mechanism, where reasonably, good medical care is provided to the poor people. Health care spending and upgrading the facilities and the management under government hospitals are a crying need of our country, to meet the needs of the poor citizens of our nation.

We also saw, that the availability of doctors in rural areas is negligible, only 2% of all allopathic doctors are rendering their services in the rural areas. A massive infusion of funds and expertise and creation of infrastructure for hospitals in the rural areas are called for. It is also seen that in the population 90% of them prefer allopathic to the traditional AYUSH (Ayurveda, yoga, umami, siddha and homoeopathic treatment).

Apart from this there is a huge shortage of doctors, and hospitals beds in comparison to our population. Unless, the government picks up the spending on health to 4 to 5% of GDP, the minimum creation of health services and infrastructure is not possible. And as a nation are, we not having the capability and the expertise in creating medical care and medical facilities, needed for our Bharat, are we lacking in any way? The only thing missing is the will and the awareness and the purpose, to which the government needs to allocate its funds on top priority. India can create the best government owned medical care in the world!" With the inhouse talent, expertise and resources available at its disposal. Medical care should be an area of prime focus for our nation.

We look at other advanced economies, the quality and quantity of medical facilities available are admirable, and that too, it is provided by the Government as strong institutions worthy of its name, for its citizens. The Social security net surrounding medicine, is admirable in other developed nations such as the UK, USA, Japan, Saudi, Europe, Australia, to name a few. All the medical infrastructure is mostly government run and monitored and provision of medical services remains free in these economies. They are admirable! Does our country India lack anything in any way, including the resources, the Doctors or expertise in mirroring this state of affairs in our nation? All over the world, the best of Doctors we know very well are Indians, Indian Doctors abroad are the most respected and reputed, why have they not given their service to our nation, being Indians? The reason is obvious, it is the current state of affairs in the medical field in our nation. It is time for a massive call to action from our Government of India, to provide not only the social security net, but the best medical infrastructure and Medical services to the citizens of India!

And free of cost to the benefit of the poor!

Chapter 12

Restoring Ecological Balance of Our Planet and Halting Environmental Degradation

We all know the problems we humans have created for ourselves, by the wanton exploitation of the natural resources, in a non-sustainable, and non-renewable manner, and in the process polluting the environment in a manner causing and creating harm not only to human existence, but all the other species of living beings including all animal and plant life on our Mother earth.

We need to understand that our Mother earth on which we exist with all other species, is the greatest gift, of God and is the most precious possession we have as humans. We humans have value of precious stones and metals, but are we so unaware of the most precious thing we have? Our Mother earths? We were gifted our Mother earth to live and enjoy by God, whereas not realising this truth we have taken this most precious gift for granted, and started polluting and damaging it in such a way, that our very existence has come under question as a species, dragging with it, the destiny of all life, on this planet-all plant and animal life into a question mark. We have acted irresponsibly and unwisely, in utilising the resources of our Mother earth, in our mad rush to create materialistic wealth, for human comfort and for the mad rush in quest of our sensory pleasure's fulfilment.

We have and still do, waste a lot of our natural resources, which are turning scarce, as we plunder them wantonly. And unless we stop the destructive process we have started, and reverse the degradation of our planet, we endanger the survival of all life on this planet including ours, and the day we witness this, is not far to come!

Since we created the problems, we need to find our own solutions, and the Irony of us is that, we know the solutions to the problems we have created, well to most of them, and we need to just implement such solutions to solve our problems, and to reverse the destructive process to a constructive one, only the awareness and the will to implement them is lacking, and not known to the authorities who can execute the remedial actions already known.

First let us list out the problems, and then discuss the solutions to them, to be implemented by those having the authority to do so. The problems are manifold in nature, firstly, we need to stop the depletion of our water bodies, in the rivers, by re-forestation of our land, as the trees and plants are not only the chief source of oxygen for the breathing and survival needs of not only humans, but all animal life. Apart from the production of oxygen for our survival, the trees and plant life, it also is the chief source of feeding the below surface ground water, and as the ground water resources are connected to the rivers, they feed the rivers with water as well, and the river waters, are the main sources of drinking water to us humans, but also all animal life on our planet. The rate at which how much of the forest cover has already depleted is a cause for worry, and even more urgent, we need to call a halt to further depletion of the forest cover right away, or else the already depleted water resources will, cause starvation of drinking water of alarming proportions.

When people find water scarcity, the scenario becomes very alarming indeed. Water is necessary for our survival, as well as the survival of both plant and animal life. The desert like environmental creation will starve the growing population of our world. And with it scarcity of oxygen producing forests, will ensure, we inhale large quantities of polluted air we have created by the way we have industrialised our land, and inhaling polluted air will cause all sorts of damage and diseases to our human body, and death to all plant and animal life on an unprecedented scale, a form of destruction to all life on our planet, as the ecological balance of the planet is disturbed.

So, the immediate solution is to cause re-forestation, to retain and replenish our water resources, and to allow the air to remain sufficiently pure, by creation of oxygen, and limiting the consumption of air which is polluted, and one of the main causes of diseases and destruction of plant and animal life on our Mother earth.

As far as replenishing and filling the void created by water depletion, which has already made water scarce in our world, the immediate remedy, with the help of advanced technology is to convert the sea water which is abundant, to drinking water, by a special process of filtration which is available, which removes the salt and other impurities from the sea or ocean water, converting it to drinking water suitable for human consumption. This technology was developed by Manchester University in UK, and the filtration material is called 'A Graphene Sieve,' made of very tiny carbon composites.

As for river water purification and ground water purification, separate technology is available to deal with polluted waters, and industrial waste disposal in an eco-friendly manner, through Japanese technology, which either recycles or processes industrial waste, to convert it to chemicals which will not pollute the environment and is recyclable too. These factory- plants also purify polluted water, especially river waters. This is a good solution to purify our rivers and to create pure drinkable water from ocean waters on a large scale to meet the demands of water of humans who are dying or suffering from lack of drinking water in our country.

We see a lot of waste of plastic used for different purposes, from water bottle cans, to cutlery, packaging, to storage, etc., but the plastic we use is not biodegradable. The first step to be taken in this regard is to stop the production of such plastic, which is not only polluting our land, but our oceans at an alarming pace. For us humans, the harmful plastic is a source of pollution, which has a direct relation to polluting our environment which occurs through dumping plastic trash. Large quantities of harmful plastics are also hurting our marine life, causing large-scale destruction in our ocean waters, thereby causing the death and destruction of all marine life, which in an alarming fashion is disturbing the ecological balance of our planet.

The solution to pollution caused by plastic waste is three- fold. Firstly, we need to popularise the use of biodegradable plastics for all our domestic and industrial consumption. These types of plastic will become part of the earth's surface, a very short time after their disposal. So, we need to immediately ban the use of polluting plastic for all the purposes it is used for currently. Secondly, we need to recycle the harmful plastics which have already been produced, to use as raw material in making our roads, or they can be converted to Bio fuel. As Bio fuel, they will not pollute the environment, and when plastic is used as a raw material in making roads, it not only reduces and recycles the bad plastic, but the roads' quality is superb, and the damage due to bad weather conditions causing road damages is checked to a large extent.

Especially these new roads will not be damaged by the onslaught of rains and other harsh weather conditions, we not only save money and effort in having roads repaired, but also, the plastics are re-used in a beneficial way to serve our own purpose. A third initiative is to do a large-scale clean up, of all the plastic dumped into the oceans, already environment friendly individuals on their own, and some private organisations and some of the government states, have initiated action to clean up the oceans, by collecting all the plastic trash dumped on a large scale, and efforts are being to recycle this collected plastics from our seas and oceans, giving life survival space to our valuable marine life. The important thing is to create the awareness of this and involve organisations and nations to take up this task by scaling up the activity to collect the plastic waste from our oceans. These three initiatives will halt the environmental degradation caused by plastic pollution in a swift fashion.

Next is rubber and leather goods disposal, causing environmental pollution. Although leather is a natural raw material, it is the chemical treatment which is given to it in factories to make them of commercial use, when leather is disposed of normally, it is a cause of large-scale chemical pollution which can harm all life; that is the problem. Apart from that, production of leather causes, more large-scale animal Slaughter which again disturbs the ecological balance in our environment, between plant and animal life on our planet. Already, technology and knowhow exist to recycle leather for re-use by the people, by processing old used leather at such factories, to save and cut down on the use of leather, by recycling the leather profitably, by some of the organisations who are already doing this. We only need to create awareness of this technology, and scale up this activity of recycling leather goods, meant normally for disposal. This may not solve the issue but will reduce the intensity of the problem created by leather goods disposal.

Secondly, all rubber products can be converted to a source of bio-fuel by processing it with a technology available for the same. We see a lot of pollution occurring due to disposal and dumping of rubber products, so if converted to bio-fuel, such fuel permanently disposes of the rubber which could have turned into toxic waste on its disposal normally. The technology for this is available, some pioneering companies are already doing this activity, we just need to create the awareness to tackle the problem of rubber waste and scale up this activity.

Then comes the pollution caused by cars, and other types of automobiles, by the toxic emissions, which are coming as exhaust gases from our automobiles. Well, the needs for transportation, will increase with time further. And if all our cars are powered by fossil fuels, then the level of air pollution will make this planet very inhospitable for us in the not so far future. But the automobile industry has given good thought to this problem, and now the use of electric vehicles is on the rise. Even in our nation, the prime minister has launched initiatives for making and running all types of automobiles electric. This will soon solve the problem of power for transportation needs. China has made great progress in the development and practical use of electric vehicles in their nation, we need to emulate them, and have a technical collaboration with them to get the technology transfer and make the use of electric cars spread across our nation, and the world, to eliminate the pollution created by fossil fuels in the transportation sector.

A big source of pollution comes because of our needs for power for many of our purposes, the first among and chief of them being electrical power. Which runs our homes, offices, factories and what not. Solar energy has been a partial alternative for pollution free electrical production of power. But has proven to be only a partial success due to its limitations till date. But a leading scientist in the US feels that solar power is the only good and viable alternative to energy production for our future. According to Elon Musk, it would take the size of a small portion of land about 100 square miles of a solar power generator to power the entire United States of America! With storage batteries to occupy space of an additional 1 Square miles! He also says this must combine with roof-top solar at home and utility solar to make the entire United States' power production free from any polluting emissions! Though this is an ambitious vision, it underlines the technological importance attached today in choosing solar power as an alternate energy source to power generated from, polluting technology, such as fossil fuels and nuclear energy. It would be a good idea, if our government subsidised the cost of solar panels, and generators to be used in each home, with some incentives attached to reduce our nation's dependence on other polluting sources of power production. And the vision shared by the scientist and innovator Elon Musk is put to a feasibility test for implementation.

We all know that lots of our food, both vegetarian and non-vegetarian, get disposed of as waste, this not only causes a large amount of wastage of food, but also, it creates lots of waste, which needs to be dumped off, and this dumped off food waste is a cause for growth of diseases and infections of all types in us humans and emission of harmful gases too. So, what do we do about this? Fortunately, there is a solution for this also; we have a technology, which converts all food waste into manure in a matter of a day or 24 hours, as it is processed by this machine. These machines can be placed in all homes and restaurants, hotels, for efficient and beneficial disposal off food waste. When food is converted this way to manure for farming or to plant trees, it is by far the richest source of manure for our food cultivation and for planting trees. This also reduces the need for use of harmful fertilisers for growing our food, which are manufactured in factories using chemicals, which again cause and are a source of pollution. In fact, this type of manure can be sold to the farmers, who will reap a rich harvest with this type of manure, which is full of humus material necessary for good farming and enhances the quality of top soil, for the plants and trees. The name of this innovative machine and technology is Zera Food, recycler of whirlpool corporation, invented by W-labs in the company. This process of creation of manure from food waste is called food composting, however the traditional food composting methods are very cumbersome, and attract pests, as the whole process of composting usually takes anywhere from three to six months. But through this new technology and machine, food composting is convenient, food is converted to manure only in 24 hours! Which is a good alternative to dumping food, which also pollutes our environment and causes infections and pests. They can be commercially produced and bought by all households, who can then sell the manure for a price to the farmers for their farming needs.

These are some of the major problems highlighted to tackle environmental damage and ecological imbalance and some innovative solutions and action points to reverse the degradation of our natural resources, which if not checked on a war footing, will lead to ills like climate change, which is the main cause of rising temperatures, and melting glaciers threatening our world and the depletion of the ozone layer which protects us from the harmful rays of the sun.

We need to treat our Mother Earth as the most precious thing we have for our survival, the best gift that God gave us for us to live and enjoy. We cannot take it for granted anymore, and we need to take immediate steps like the ones described to restore the ecological balance, to enjoy our world with peace and joy prevailing on our Mother Earth! A blessed and blissful existence on our planet mutually with the animal and plant life thriving as the beauty of life with us!

Chapter 13

Can We Call an End to Crime, Violence on Our Mother Earth? Is It Possible? I Think So

Once one of the greatest sages of India, Lord Buddha said, "Do not believe what you cannot perceive or experience as truth yourself." What I am going to talk about is of such a nature.

What is the root cause of crime and violence? Who commits crime and violence in society? Obviously, it is the individual, and when it is a group of them, it is called organised crime who are violent in nature. Why do individuals or a group of individuals commit crime? The answer to this is a two-step process on how individuals turn into criminals.

The first important fact about them is that they have no or very little control over their sense organs or their mind. Living thus as their animate tendencies, become prominent, in their behaviour. So thus, they live a life without awareness and consciousness. Obviously, this is happening to them, because they are ignorant of the process of life, and the true nature of our existence. Their acts are compulsive in nature and are driven by the situations they face, and the way they react to it, on impulse.

The first truth that they are not aware of is the importance of establishing total control over their sense organs. Further, they are not aware of the right purpose to which they must put their sex organs to. That is, it is meant only for procreation or giving birth. They are drawn into the vicious cycle of acquisition of sensory pleasures, and in this race, they commit several crimes, which is like a vortex of pain and pleasure, which is snapping away their life, to end in ruin and later their death, either through diseases or through the rule of law. Fear and suspicion are a constant companion driving their lives.

Well, having no control over their animal tendencies, the positive and subtle process of yoga also, which enhances one's awareness and consciousness, and its benefits are very far from them. As they are trapped in seeking carnal pleasures, which becomes the very basis of their life and existence.

But being a human is not the same as being an animal. Humans are endowed with an almost unsurpassable and unlimited intellect, and the mind is a very powerful tool under a human's disposal. If it is not controlled, it can do irreparable damage, to the self, and other humans around them. Animals, on the other hand, have limitations. Once their hunger is satisfied, they have reached their goal and so go no further. They do not carry an infinitely capable intellect, which characterises a human being.

Satisfying hunger or ensuring survival is important for a human, but then, that is just the beginning of his desires. The animate tendencies or animal spirits, come with an insurmountable ego, jealousy, anger, hatred, pride, greed, selfishness, lack of empathy or compassion, rudeness, possessiveness, carelessness, tendency to exploit, dependence on intoxicants to subvert their nerves, and all types of antisocial or inhuman behaviours, one can think of.

Many such individuals, living an ignorant existence, such as this, are led to crime, and violent behaviour is common to them. Rudeness is their second nature. They try to evade the law and the police, or enforcement authorities. Ultimately, law catches on to them. To them, the value of the life of any human, are lower than and less important than the acquisition of sensory pleasures or materialistic wealth. Their intellect, their minds become their worst enemy, with it they not only cause harm to themselves but to other fellow human beings, who suffer due to them.

So, what do we do to such people who have become anti-social elements, and most of them are free, damaging society, and its structure? The way the structure of our society is built today, the only way society tries to stop or discourage such people, is recourse to punishment based on a legal framework. But does this work, it only curbs crime and violence, it does not stop it. It's only a way to maintain some sort of order by instilling fear in such people. But is that the real solution, does crime and violence, really come under control and subside, with this reactive strategy? Does the rate of crime committed come down, and is this really a solution to this problem?

Obviously, punishment and legal process alone is no solution. It does not stop or resolve the situation, rather, the criminals, use their intellect to bypass the legal system, as we advance in technology, and the life process evolves and gets more complex, the criminals get more advanced in perpetuating crime, breaking the law, and escaping punishment, and still commit the crimes, unabated. They try not to be caught by the police; they fool the authorities, by escaping punishment wantonly, to commit further crimes and violent acts of defiance. Clearly, this is no solution, and the legal system and the entire social framework designed to curb crime, is a failure, and nowhere near reaching their objectives. The crime rate goes up and up only, and the rate of crimes increase, with the growth in population in the nation.

So then, is there a real solution to this social problem? Is there a way to control or stop crime almost completely, and banish it from the face of our Mother Earth?

Yes, there is, obviously, as for every problem, there is a solution given by God, our Creator. A two-pronged approach is necessary. First, we must not allow the disease to take root; it should be nipped in the bud. It is said that prevention is better than cure. Well, in an early stage of life, age appropriate, children should be trained and educated and made to realise the truth about life. As they reach and cross their puberty and their hormones attack their intellect, they should be taught on how to control their palate, told about the rightful use of their organs meant for procreation and explained about the pitfalls of quests over sensory pleasures. They should be educated about the purpose of marriage, and how they can be joyful and live blissfully and happily, holding their responsibility, whilst having and raising their own family, whilst following the Bram Acharya vrat in their married lives.

And the second part of this process, equally important, that apart from this education, they should be taught inner engineering, or the science of knowing their inner self, and the truth about the true nature of our existence. The yoga training causes them to reach their pinnacle of awareness and consciousness and makes them realise the responsibility they carry towards society being human, and arms them, with the ability to respond as a human fully. Unless these two processes are followed through, by each child coming to the school, which focuses on both inner engineering and external engineering, that is, the science of the inner self and the physicality of our existence.

No individual or child should be allowed to enter the formal society, as an adult, to take up his responsibility in our society, till they reach this type of awareness and consciousness. The pass certificate to enter formal society should be given to only those students who are fully aware and are conscious. This 2-step process for everyone guarantees that no individual will turn out into a liability to society, and will ensure he is an asset to the human community. Once this formal system is established, these adults will not be failures, and the rate of crime will drop to near zero.

Nothing like this has ever been done before, so it takes time to establish this new order of things in our society. The very nature of us humans needs to change and be reformed. But there are those in our society, who have already graduated from school, entered our formal society. Most of them are leading a credible life, but a large percentage are living a life of hopelessness, have turned their lives to failures, and many have turned into criminals, and have become violent, causing havoc and have turned into the primary reason for chaos in our society already. What do we do of such people?

Firstly, this process needs to be made public, and it should become mainstream knowledge, the nature and the benefits of both inner and external engineering, to each member of our society. Secondly, those of whom, have become extreme cases, they are either in jail, or in psychiatric wards, being punished for their crimes, or being treated for the misbalance which comes with leading a life remaining uneducated, a life devoid of awareness and consciousness, to them, and with them a formal agreement should be reached, they need to be educated on the science of the inner self, and the external sciences, to make them normal. This applies to those who are physically fit otherwise, and it is possible to impart knowledge in them, and they are physically capable of learning.

I am sure most criminals serving a sentence of long years in jail can be reformed by training and teaching them the truth about life. But those of whom, who are charged with homicide, and are convicted, and face a death sentence, this relief efforts cannot apply to them. For other crimes, if they face long years of confinement in prison, as their punishment, I do not see why they cannot be reformed, and after the educational and training process is complete, they may be granted a leave from their jails, on the merit of good conduct, a bit early. The success of this process on them is the only basis; their jail term may be reduced from the years already pronounced by law.

To those who are languishing in mental hospitals, and are diagnosed with psychiatric problems, a combination of medicines to get them into a stable condition may be needed, before they are formally taught the science of the inner self, to reform them, and to make them conscious and aware of the truth of our nature of existence, and once they become normal, and are balanced, allowed to enter the formal society again.

The process of those, who are adults, who need such help, to help them, reform them, make them normal needs to be done on a warlike footing, as this is the only true way to end criminal and violent behaviour.

The process to be established for children and teenagers should be concrete, so that the entire process of criminalisation of the society slowly comes to an end. And for those in jails or mental hospitals, the required effort from the formal society needs to be put, to end crime and violence, and to give them a second chance at life.

Doing this would set a precedent not yet established in society, the very knowledge, that such a formal process exists to deliver them from their misery, itself, would set an example to society, and all the adults, who are in the middle zone, only half conscious of the truth, it would motivate them, to practice both the sciences, especially the science of learning, perceiving and experiencing the truth about their inner self, and about life, would make the endeavour successful.

Word of mouth and prime examples of this process and the benefits to human wellbeing realising and leading to true happiness, joy, blessedness, and blissfulness will be a strong motivator to bring about these changes in our society and for our humanity for all eternity to come.

To recount an occurrence in the great life of Buddha, in our sacred land of Bharat: We can never forget the life example of Angulimal, one of the most pious disciples of Lord Buddha. He was a very ferocious demon-like criminal, whom the Buddha encountered in his life, only to reform him, show him the truth of life, and turn him into a Holy Saint, like him. If this result could be achieved back then, so many thousands of years back, does it not serve as an example to us, to repeat it on a larger scale, in our modern world, surely, since we know how it happened, and we know how to achieve it for us, why not now, emulate Buddha, the great one, in our modern society today, of what he achieved for Angulimal?

I am sure once this process is implemented, the criminals will not only thank us but hold us in veneration and give their blessings to us all! And love us for delivering them out of their misery and giving them a chance to live again. So, will those patients in mental hospitals, getting a second chance at life! Their blessings alone, I think, would be enough as a return to society's efforts put in for them! To give a cure to the malaise that ails us today! May God bless us all! And Godspeed us to achieve these noblest of intentions!

Chapter 14

What Is a Happy Marriage and Family? the Success of the Institution of Marriage and Family, as a Unit of Our Life

Well, since the beginning, all couples marry with an aim to live together happily ever after, well in all marriage ceremonies conducted following any religious faith, this is the solemn and sacred pledge all couples take in the name of God.

But we witness, something else happens after marriage, among most couples, and if they have children, the children to suffer if there is acrimony between the husband and the wife. The problem is usually a lack of understanding between the husband and wife, and this leads to quarrelling.

Well, in India, the quarrel, is tolerated by the wife, who compromises, for the sake of the family, and bends to the wishes of her husband, to let the marriage remain sacrosanct, and the same behaviour is also encouraged in our nation, by the society, as in our culture, the marriage ceremony, and the marriage relationship, is considered as a very important institution, which is the basic unit of the way, we live our lives. It is not to be violated. At least this is true for most of our nation.

But now in our modern society, we have started emulating, the western culture, and the women, at least in the cities, as educated individuals, have become independent, and do not tolerate the differences they have with their spouse, anymore, and since a legal recourse is available, divorce is the option, taken up by many couples, as the last option, destroying our age old institution of marriage and family. While in the western culture, marriage itself is rare, and the institution of marriage has been demolished in most of the population, in the west.

Well, the effects of a separation between married couples, if they have had children, is a bit tragic, as children suffer a lot, due to the quarrelling of their parents, and their failure, a break in the family unit, has a deep and debilitating impact, if children must face their parents quarrelling, and eventually break up. Even in couples without children, the path of divorce takes a heavy psychological and emotional toll on the married couple also, as they separate.

What is generally the reason for failed marriages, leading to failure in the institution of family as a unit? The blaming game between husband and wife, to watch itself, is a tragic occurrence for them the children, as well as for the family. If the couple separate, without giving birth to children, the problem is not compounded, but if the separation occurs, after the birth of children, both for the couple, and more so for the children, the heart break is too traumatic to bear for their entire life time. Especially, the effects of a separation, takes a very heavy toll on the children, who at a tender age go through unbearable emotional and mental suffering, it also impacts their future life, and the way they grow up and survive! For the children, it's a punishment given by their parents, usually to sometimes last for their lifetime. In the Indian culture, where the family function as a unit of life, is very basic, and any breakage of the family unit, is usually a very heart rendering experience, both for those who go through it, and for the relatives also, and the friends of the family to witness.

Well, why do separations and divorces ever happen, the marriage councillors, usually fail to stop it. The reason for divorces is of a primary nature. The acrimony and fighting occurs, and the pain of it comes, because, the married couple, are ignorant to the basic process of life. First, they need to be aware about, why did they marry? Well, they married out of love or to develop love in the relationship and the family, who wanted to live happily ever after. In India, most of the marriages, do not break, just because, of sentiments attached to the family as a unit. Which is a great thing. However, while the family, remains united, the friction between the couple continues, and even though the separation has been avoided, for a large part of the married life, the quarrelling continues, unabated, and this is also taken for as granted by our society as normal between husband and the wife, while this state of affairs takes a heavy toll on the children, who remain as witness to the on-going tragic drama, in their home.

So, then what is the solution for this problem, which has reached epidemic proportions in our Indian society and culture and abroad? Well, in a marriage, although the legal sanction is given, the pursuit of sensory pleasures becomes the primary objective between the husband and wife. And the right to it seems to be licenced here, in marriages. The same problem already mentioned before—the organs to give birth are meant to be used for procreation and are only meant for giving birth to the Offspring to build a happy family and are not to be used as means of experiencing sensual pleasures.

Once the husband and wife start indulging in the wrong practice, the animate tendencies in both arise, leave alone loss of health for them both, the marriage transforms in to a slanging match, of one trying to score points over the other. Ego takes birth between them, which is a disruptive animate tendency. Quarrels start over doing the normal chores of the house, as for both of them, it becomes irritating, as both their bodies become incapable of doing work, and they start finding things stressful, then the fight between rights, from money, to fighting over influencing their children, and as the animate tendencies rise, open brawling becomes the order of the day, as the husband may start abusing or beating his wife, and they both tend to ill-treat their children!

So, then what is the solution for this, obviously, the solution lies in giving up the pursuit of sensory pleasures, and adopting the practice of Bram Acharya Vrat, even as they continue to remain householders, and a closely-knit family. And among some couples, if they have not developed the control over their sense organs then to do so immediately, before the marriage turns into a failure, and the children are affected badly, out of their animate behaviour. The three-step process explained needs to be followed to establish the potency for Good Karma.

When the animate tendencies drop because of following the Bram Acharya Vrat, all those teething problems, like ego, and the various reasons which were leading to fights will dissolve, as the body of both, will recover from illness and the capacity for work comes back, so all the reasons which the real cause of quarrels were will go away. The focus then shifts to the upbringing of their children, the right type of loving and caring atmosphere returns to the home. The children are set good examples by their parents' behaviour and their handling. They start excelling in their studies at school, and they feel loved and nurtured at their home. The children develop equilibrium in their behaviour and character, winning the praise of their friends and relatives. A very positive and constructive atmosphere is created at home. The home and the family become like a Temple, with this kind of merit full and blessed living.

Well, there is a second step—that is the duty of the parents in a family, bearing children as their responsibility. They need to teach the children, the same basic knowledge, which they know and have lived in their life, so that, their children at an early stage in life, get a good start to their life and are ready to enter the formal society, with confidence and sure guaranteed success. They need to know the importance of gaining the control over their sensory organs, by exercising control over their palate, the important point to be made to them, is the knowledge of the rightful use of the organs for procreation, what they are meant for, and then, they should be taught the science of the inner self, or inner engineering, or yoga, and they must taste the benefit of full awareness and consciousness being established, with the guidance of their parents. The parents, who love their children, are responsible to make their children also as responsible citizens of our nation, and the ability to respond to life, with success, is the chief responsibility of the parents of the children, apart from providing the learning of the external sciences, or conventional education. A parent always wants to feel proud of their children, well, the tools to ensuring that, is in the hand of the parents, who are the source of the main influence and caring in the lives of their children. It is the first duty of any responsible parent, to equip the child with those qualities which are admirable to all of society.

A parent need not leave lots of wealth or savings behind for their children, as their gift whilst they depart. The only precious gift any parent must ensure for their child is to educate them with the basic knowledge of life, and to ensure, they leave behind responsible children, who are sufficiently empowered to take care of their own responsibility and can confidently take care of themselves in the world they have been bought by consciously as their parents in the first place. This is the greatest and the only truly worthy gift a loving parent must leave behind or give their children. This would surely be the best blessing a loving parent can give to his children!

Chapter 15

Why Are We Born, and Where Do We? Come From? and After Death Where Do We Go?

a. Our Ancient Indian wisdom says-Believe only that, which you can perceive and experience as truth in your own life. Do not believe anyone or any source of knowledge, unless you experience the truth.

b. Is it true that we came to this world with nothing? and similarly we will go back with nothing? We took birth in our mother's womb, took a part of the earth offered there, grew into a baby, took birth, ate food as part of the earth, and literally from the beginning of our birth manufactured our body and our mind from the earth, so is it not obvious we are beyond the body and our mind? And when we depart, we shed this earth, which we accumulated, as a loan, and give it back when we die?

c. when we die what goes with us? Not even our name, so name and fame also become irrelevant to us after our death. But what we surely take with us after our death is our karmic account. If we have done good karma it goes with us, and if bad, that also goes with us once we die. Based on our karmic account we are re-born; into the circumstances we find ourselves in our next birth. If with good karma, we are born in privileged, in favourable circumstances, if with past bad karma, we are born in difficult or unfavourable circumstances.

d.   In our life, all people are born with a new karmic slate to write their life on and create the karmic account for the current life. The law of Karma makes life a level playing field, it makes us all equal. A privileged person can fall from grace with bad karma, and similarly, with good karma, in life, even a poor and suffering person can rise in grace so much so that the whole world will applaud in appreciation! and he can be a source of inspiration for all!

e.   It is this body and mind we manufactured that separates one living being or a human from another. Since our body takes the form of a shape, a shape derived from the earth, we used, to manufacture our body and mind, That is the cause of the difference between one human from another, so essentially minus the body and the mind, we are all one- the union between all humans and living beings is here, in the soul of each human. Our oneness happens thus, as part of the same creator. The moment we shed the body and mind we manufactured from this earth, this shape dissolves as we die, we are one and the same, as part of the creator, without the body and the mind. Our union is thus so simple for all humans and living beings.

f.   Why are we born? How come we are born? Where did we come from? The answer to this is very simple, we as part of the creator, or you can take it-the creator decided to take birth, to wexperience and enjoy life in this form. So, we are born, we took birth to manufacture this body, solely because we wanted to. That was our will. So simple. Why did we choose to be born? It is because we wanted to experience and enjoy life. It is that simple. Where do we come from? The same source-the creator- of whom we are a part. So, in other words the creator wanted to experience life and enjoy it like this, so we were born. And so, as we die once we live and experience this life, we return to where we all come from-the same source-the creator himself or God. We only seem separate, because our body and mind we manufactured, seem different, due to our thoughts and our shapes. Otherwise minus this, we are one and the same. Even the earth we used to manufacture this body, is also the same, the difference is only our individual perception of life.

g. Then you might ask, that does not explain all the truth. What then, this non-living matter that surrounds us? Where did this come from? Is this not separate from us living beings? For this we need to answer one fundamental question- will all this non-living matter in this world, exist, if we were not there to perceive it as living beings? It would not exist or have any significance, if we were not there to experience it. So, the whole of creation and the creator is one only. So, this non-living matter was created by the creator, or us, we as part of the creator, so that we can experience and enjoy life! So, this whole non-living matter is part of us, created by the creator to experience life! So, the non-living matter was created with a purpose-it was created by the creator to experience life! And the creator experiences life and enjoys life through us human or living beings. This non-living matter is a bed-rock of all creation! That's all!

h. Then what is love, caring, empathy, compassion we feel for each other? Well it is nothing but the expression amongst us we have as a language to express our oneness. It is the expression of our union, which is basic to the true nature of our existence. We are all one, and since we seem separated only by this body and mind, that we ourselves manufactured to experience life, love, caring, empathy, compassion, is the way we express our oneness to each other. Thus, the language of love and caring for each other -is truly the language of God-or the creator. So Good and evil also happen the same way, through this-when we are conscious -we express our love or oneness for each other, when we are not conscious or do not know the truth about life, are ignorant to the truth about life, we are bad, not recognizing the oneness- or love, that characterizes our very existence, we turn against each other or do bad karma and harm each other, by either thought, deed, or words, which is what we call as bad. So Good and Bad happen in our life like this. This is the secret of good and bad karma.

i. Then comes the question, did the creator or God have any beginning or end? We seem to have it? Well the answer to this question is obvious-our lives have a beginning and an end, as we are born, and we die, our self-manufactured body and mind, but how can the creator or God have a beginning or end. The very nature of the creator is infinite, all his creation is infinite in nature-Thus the creator or we as a part of him, have no beginning or end, by our very nature, we are infinite, so is all the non-living matter that surrounds us. The creator never came into existence, since it is infinite, nor is there an end to the creator due to infinity. The creator was always there and will always be there, as infinite. We who manufactured this body and mind are similarly infinite, but the body and the mind we manufactured for ourselves to experience life, if finite-it is born and it dies. As we shed our body our perceived end comes, which is finite by its very nature. We know no death, being a part of the creator, it is our body and mind which perish, after having our experience of life!

j. What about the purpose of our life? What do we do with life? Why this effort to be born? Well we wanted to experience life, and we took birth to celebrate our existence. How do we celebrate our existence? as part of the creator? well we want to feel happy, joyful, blissful, peaceful, successful, and most importantly, we want to enjoy our experience of life! Would we ever do anything in our life, if we do not enjoy it? We would be wasting our life, if we did so! So basically, everybody wants to enjoy life to the fullest! Basically, we manufactured our body and mind to experience enjoyment in our finite life! We would not waste a moment of this life, doing things that does not give us enjoyment, is that not true? This is the purpose of life! And what we wanted to do with our life! It is to enjoy life! So simple! How can we truly enjoy life? Well it is not by deriving and experiencing sensual pleasures, as most would think, true enjoyment to any human can only happen, when he loves and cares for another human or living being, expressing the oneness, True enjoyment comes by helping another living feel happy! And perusing enjoyment in the form of acquisition of sensual pleasures, is only a form of suffering, and not enjoyment of life! It is also true, that when you help remove suffering of another, help another, it is the true God blessed genuine enjoyment of life. This is the only true way to enjoy life-to love and to care for another! Thus, re-enforcing in us the oneness of all!

k. Then what is this evolution we witness in our life, Well, we get better at manufacturing our body, as time goes by, since, we find more sophisticated methods to experience and enjoy life! It enriches our life further! We discover better ways to enjoy life, as we take and make better use of non-living matter, which is also of an infinite in nature. We evolve, because, we want a better experience and enjoyment of our life's and with us the technology of living-that is non-living matter we advance, as time goes further. So, the way we live to experience life, changes completely, we evolve our body and mind, as this evolve, our handling of non-living matter also evolves, through the advancement in technology.

1. Then what is this over- population thing? It needs to be controlled? Well we are unconsciously or consciously increasing our population. The problem is the entire humanity is not fully conscious on this issue, and we as part of the ultimate Brahman, are increasing the population without realizing that the resources on our mother earth are limited, and will exhaust if population is not controlled. We are conscious as individuals, but not conscious as one humanity, so those who hold power need to take preventive measures to bring the population under control, there is still time, for the population explosion to hit our daily lives on our mother earth, but we need to start correcting the situation right away, to avoid that eventuality.

So, this is to conclude my answer to some basic questions of our life, in my experienced and perceived life, what I found to be the truth in my life.

Chapter 16

The Divine Language of God: Why Do We Miss This Magic in Our Life Foolishly?

What is the Divine language of God? Try to guess it! Of course, the Divine language of God are words spoken out of Love, respect and caring!

It is a language with magic, whenever you use it, it will never fail you in your life. It is God himself who gave us this language, we use it very sparingly, and many times forget to use it at all. We forget the Divine language.

Of all languages known to man, this is the greatest language, and if you use it, victory will always be yours in this world. When you speak out of love, respect and caring, show some responsibility towards others, you can take it for granted, that God is speaking through you. So, your purpose is achieved. Well the purpose has to worthy as well to use this language.

We come across many conflicts with others in our life, we generally fight to win, but suppose, you give up fighting, and instead speak out of love, respect and caring to the opposite person, just see what will happen!, the magic starts working, he responds out of love and respect too and then, surprisingly, you both find an amicable and loving solution acceptable to both of you, and friendship starts developing, and the matter is resolved amicably and easily to each other's satisfaction!

You come across a person, who is rude and he may even be a criminal, no matter what the state of a human being, well you must be careful, that you do not expose yourself to harm, but you just try it, when you are face to face to this person, speak out of love and respect, show some caring, and lo! Behold! The magic starts happening, in spite of a bad record, the opposite person starts reciprocating in return, and you will be amazed!

This is a prime example of the Divine language of God working to the very best and its high impact in our world!

Let me give you a example of peace & love from a actual incident in our life, which impacted the whole world forever, and can be seen reverberating and influencing humanity always even now! This has set the GOLD Standard in Humanity and teaches us the true meaning of what it is being a Human!

I am talking of none other than Mahatama Gandhi, a name I am sure every human knows about in our world! The main teaching of Mahatama Gandhi, are coined in One word described by him-Ahimsa! Ahimsa means non-violence! Ahimsa also teaches us of living in Peace, Love, Kindness, Caring, Prosperity and Happiness! This applies to the Individual, the family, the Society, the Nations and finally our World, Living as One Family, and values defining all relationships! This are the teachings of the Mahan Atma! Which means Divine Soul! One of the greatest among men! M.K. GANDHI!

Mahatma Gandhi, is also the Father of the Nation-India! Though the whole world hold's him in reverance. particularly Africa, where he had spent a part of his life, leaving behind the same teachings!

It is Mahatma Gandhi who taught us the language of God! Which is Love!

Mahatma practised Ahimsa, against the British colonization of India, and Gandhi Practised Ahimsa, and without lifting a Sword, the entire Nation together forced the British to leave India, and Mahatma Gandhi got the Independence for India, with his followers! This is unprecedented in History and the World! If you want to know all about it, read Mahatma Gandhi's Autobiography "The story of my Experiments with Truth". You may also watch the movie made and directed by Sir Richard Attenbourough, it is based on the life of M.K.GANDHI, the movie "Gandhi", to feel the true language of God-Which is the language of LOVE!

Just you remember this language of God, and use it as much as possible in our world, in your life, just see how effortless and easy your life becomes! Remember, never to forget this truth about life, remember it every moment, in your life, and use it well and always, and true worthwhile victory will be yours always! This is also the Goal of life-Peace, Love, Kindness, Caring, Prosperity, and True Happiness! May God bless all humanity with Ahimsa! (Non-Violence).

Chapter 17

Saving our Trees to Sustain our Life

Every time a tree is cut on our mother earth, something significant affecting our lives as humans and animal life happens.

We permanently loose a source of Oxygen that sustains our life's, for the next 12 to 15 year's! Till we plant another tree in its place and it grows again to restore our source of Oxygen which we lost.

We all know that without oxygen no human life or animal life can survive, and we also know the scorching pace at which we are cutting down the trees on our planet, without any forethought, towards the damage which we are doing to our life's.

What will happen if Oxygen percentage as a part of the air we breathe keeps going down? Automatically, the content of other gases in the air we breathe increases, which is harmful to us, and is the cause of contracting many diseases, which come with it. So, in this way we are inviting a disaster on ourselves by destroying our trees, so carelessly.

Another important part trees play is they attract rain from the clouds above us. Rain means a source of drinking water, and water for our farms, which is the main source of our food. Well you that after air, next comes water and food to sustain our life on this earth.

More over the trees also prevent soil erosion, and this is very important for the plants and vegetation, which give us our fruits and vegetables to grow on our land. Without trees the quality of the soil becomes unfit to grow vegetation and plants which is not only important for our food, but also our survival.

Another important thing about trees is that when rains come, the trees act like a sponge, and allow the rain water to percolate down into the ground water, and as we know the ground water is another source of drinking water for us humans, as well as well water, drawn by motors to irrigate our farms to grow food.

Trees which feed the ground water, and collect it, are also connected to our rivers, and feed our rivers with water. We all know the critical importance of rivers as a source of drinking water both for us humans and animal life, without which we may not survive. So, in other words, if trees are cut, rains will be scarce, the ground water may turn empty, and ultimately our rivers will die. We have already seen a large part of our rivers, dying away, receding, going dry, as the forest cover is lost, due to trees being cut down without any thoughts as to what are we doing to our earth!

So chiefly, when you cut a tree, firstly, a source of oxygen is gone permanently, till the tree is replaced, drinking water sources are affected badly, our rivers are lost, and finally our lands run dry and are parched, as eventually they become dry and unsuitable for farming, due to lack of rains, as well as absence of ground water and rivers to irrigate them for farming to grow our food. And ultimately, animals also cannot survive, due to lack of drinking water and forest cover lost, and in fact many of the species go extinct on our earth permanently, this has already happened at an alarming rate, whilst we try to save them, and animal life is also very important for the survival of us humans, as they maintain the ecological balance, and are also important for the survival of the forests and our tree cover on our mother earth.

Therefore, so delicately it is balanced, the ecology of our planet, and if we destroy one link, or make it ineffective, all life on our earth comes under grave threat.

Can't we realize the simple fact that, the lungs we breathe, from under our chest, which cannot function without oxygen, half of these lungs are actually existing or hanging in the trees, so God distributed half our lungs on the trees, which we are so carelessly decimating, without realizing, where we are leading our human and animal life, well eventually towards self-extinction and self-destruction, by creating scarcity of oxygen, water and food!

Without realizing the scheme of things, the way God made our mother earth, and intended us to live, and the delicate ecological balance we need to maintain, we are putting our very survival on this mother earth at risk by our careless ways!

We need to halt all tree destruction, and restoration of tree and forest cover by planting trees, for our own survival on the planet immediately.

Chapter 18

Saving Our Rivers of India By Linking Them

Well planting trees to save rivers, brings more benefits than that alone. However, we have seen in our nation that many rivers went dry and are dead now already, and many are on the verge of dying in our country.

So is there a way to save them, fortunately, there is with the help of technology and engineering marvel, we as humans have invented. The key words are: Interlinking rivers!

So, what is interlinking rivers? Our nation is very big in its land mass, and if we were to divide our nation into geographical areas, the north and east stand out to be areas receiving excess or surplus rainfalls to the extent that floods are common in these areas every year. Then the western and southern part of Bharat, are areas where usually there is deficit of rainfall, and floods are rare, and many parts of these areas witness droughts, and many farmers go bankrupt and commit suicide in the rural areas, so severe is the lack of rainfall, and its inadequacy in these areas. Drinking water also becomes scarce many a times, causing death to animals and humans at times also.

What if the rivers in the north and east were interlinked by big canals as water bodies to the south and the west? What would happen is, the surplus in the north-east part of the country, will serve to fill in the deficit in the south-west part of our nation. So, in the north-east floods and destruction can be avoided and in the south-west drought and water shortage can be avoided. Moreover, rivers which are drying up in any part of our nation can be fed by these canals, and we can save our rivers from drying or dying. Furthermore, water for human use, need never be a matter of scarcity, when surplus water is stored in large reservoirs. A lot of the river waters end up flowing into the sea, and precious water, which is scarce in many parts of the country, is wasted this way, before the rivers flow eventually into the sea, we harness a part of the water in reservoirs, to completely avoid water scarcity across the nation, there is enough water to drink, and there is enough water to irrigate all farmland, to grow food, and the farmers need never commit suicide, due to bankruptcy, due to lack of rains to irrigate their farm lands.

Two three more things can happen, firstly, if rivers are dying, they can immediately be revived, if rivers are dead already, and land is still available for these rivers to flow, they can be made to come alive! So, we save our rivers by interlinking our rivers across our nation.

Secondly, since the rivers are all healthy, with this network of canals, and reservoirs, a huge output of hydroelectricity for our power needs both for domestic and industrial needs can be generated in our nation.

Thirdly, these canals and water ways can be used for laying the network of inland water transportation, substituting and shedding the load on road and rail transport in our nation, and is a very cheap method to transport both cargo and passengers across our nation.

So, interlinking of rivers as a technology is not new to our world, it has been done well in the west and is a proven technological and engineering marvel in our world. The U.S., Canada, Europe, Australia etc. are nations, where interlinking of rivers has already happened, and is very successful.

Therefore I urge the government of India, to take up interlinking of rivers across our nation as an ambitious project, to do away with floods, and droughts in our nation, to solve the drinking water and irrigation needs for our food production, for meeting our power and transportation needs and for ultimately saving our rivers of Bharat!

Chapter 19

Removing Some of the Major Bottlenecks to the Rapid Economic Development of Our Nation Bharat

Removing some of the Major Bottlenecks to the rapid economic development of our nation Bharat:

What are the bottle necks to rapid economic growth and for India to transform into an advanced economy? What steps can we take to achieve that?

First of all, we need to understand that two institutions, which are the pillars of an advanced economy are very weak in our nation.

The present status of our Government schools and our Government hospitals.

We all know that both Government schools and hospitals, lack the very basic facilities to function, and the people manning and running them, are highly unskilled and are untrained to carry out their duties.

Government schools and hospitals are the building blocks of an advanced economy and a prosperous nation.

How can a nation progress when two of the most important institutions of the government are running in such a pathetic mode?

The government owned and run schools and hospitals running in the nation form 85% of all the schools and hospitals in the nation!

So, the major facilities for primary education and Medicare are run by the government of India.

So, what do we do to make both the institutions strong? The government needs to allocate a major portion of the exchequer to upgrade the facilities available at schools and hospitals. A massive drive from the government of India to also attract highly skilled teachers and doctors needs to be initiated, and more facilities need to be created to educate both school teachers and doctors and train them.

This initiative on the part of the government will lead to rapid employment, development and fuel the economic growth in our nation.

Well educated students coming out from these schools will drive the nation forward, good and adequate Medicare facilities, will mean a healthy and a nation where suffering due to poor medical facilities will come to an end. The medical industry will also catapult the nation towards development.

Mind the fact that the schools and hospitals will remain as institutions which provide institutions for free to all the citizens of India, similar to those provided in advanced nations.

Another Important initiative is to allow Multiband Retail FDI in our nation with a word of caution. We always felt that Multiband Retail FDI will destroy local small businesses in our nation, but there is a solution to this problem, if we stipulate that all raw materials and services used by these brands are to be sourced only from within India, that all factories or services they generate should be opened only in India, and no factories or raw materials or services should come from abroad, then allowing FDI in Multiband franchises, will actually, lead to growth in India, and the growth will take place to benefit farmers and the labourers of our nation.

The demand created by these multiband franchises, will ensure that farmers get a good price for their produce, and labourer's get higher wages, as demand for labour goes up. The extra production, will give more money to the poor farmers and laborious, and the extra products manufactured, in a finished condition, will fuel the growth of the GDP of our nation.

Moreover, another benefit will be transfer of latest technology into our nation, through these foreign brands, which will lead to our nation becoming competitive in making high quality products with the latest technology.

An added benefit of technology and competitiveness is, India will soon transform into an export hub like China, and earn foreign exchange just like China!

Moreover, we have the same advantages which China enjoys, or even more- we have cheap labour and cheap prices of raw material, available in our nation, which makes our high-quality exports which will come at a cheaper price! This will make us highly competitive in the International markets! This entire scenario will lead to rapid economic development of our nation, spearheading it towards becoming one out of the club of an advanced nation.

By allowing multiband Retail FDI with these special conditions, at best what do we lose? Nothing! The smaller traders have more products to choose from to sell from their outlets! Well the profits made by these foreign brands may be transferred to their respective nation's but how much is that? It will be hardly 3 to 4 % of the sales, as some of the profits will be re-invested, and some will be sent to their home country.

Is that a big price to pay for the employment generated in our country, the better price we realize for our raw materials from farmers or service or industries, the growth in the demand leading to higher GDP? Becoming an export hub, and gaining competitiveness on a global scale and in Global markets by manufacturing the best quality products with the technology transfer? Earning high amount of foreign exchange revenues by functioning as an export hub?

Restraining multiband retail is definitely a bottle neck for our nation's economy, created by a misconception in our nation, without looking up at solution's as China has done!

Another big bottleneck to growth and us becoming an advanced nation, are our loss-making public-sector companies, including our public sector banks, with their huge NPA's. Apart from those functioning parallelly in the industrial and retail sectors in our economy.

Mostly 95% of all public sector companies are either loss making or having crippling debt. And who bales them out? It is the government which writes of their debt or losses, by using taxpayer's money! We as citizens of India, pay our taxes to the government, and our hard-earned money, instead of being used for the nations development, it is wasted in writing of losses or debt of highly inefficient and mismanaged public sector companies.

What is the problem with public sector companies? They are not accountable to anybody, nor are they answerable, nor do they carry out the affairs of the company with responsibility.

Actually, the entire public sector as a concept came from the communist ideology, after Independence, from our over engagement with Russian friendship from the then leadership of our nation.

In the whole world the communist ideology has failed miserably, and even in the land it was born, it has been abolished-Russia, but we continue to suffer from this ideology in India, where as it should have met with a decent burial in our nations ideology long back, and look at the damage and wastage that has happened since then.

In the private sector, every employee is made responsible for his work, he has to work with high efficiency, as prescribed by the management of the organization, and moreover they are answerable to their shareholders, for profit generation, and there are no free meals allowed, if you generate losses or high debt, you are thrown out by the shareholders, who demand high return on the investment they have made in the company.

The sheer size of our public sector is huge, and so are losses and debt they accumulate every year!

We cannot take any sudden steps, but step by step, slowly the divestment of the public sector and its sale and transfer to the private sector should be done.

Moreover, the sale proceeds of shares held by the government and its sale to the private sector is a huge source of revenue to the government exchequer, which the government can use to invest in those activities which are beneficial to the nation.

These are some of the major bottlenecks that are stopping our nation from transforming to a wealthy and advanced economy!

Chapter 20

Cure for Depression

You should know that Depression is a serious a very serious ailment in our world, which hits people from all walks of life. 1 out of 5 in the world suffer from the disease, and 1 out of 6 in the world, have suffered from this disease sometime in their life.

When you are suffering from this ailment, you feel sad, dejected, you have lost confidence, this generally happens because the energies in your body have come down considerably and they have come to a low ebb.

Other symptoms of depression are: you don't feel like eating or you eat too much, you don't sleep enough or you sleep too much, you feel purposeless, you feel worthless, it is also difficult for you to think and concentrate and make decisions.

This is a state of a being felling absolutely useless, you are not able to work at home, or at the office, and this is what is depression.

A very serious aspect of depression is that you get thoughts of committing suicide, and we have heard that lots of people commit suicide when they are suffering from depression.

How is depression generally treated by doctor's? Medication is one, and then psychiatric help is given, and if both don't work, you are given anaesthesia, and to give you, electro convulsive shocks, electricity is passed through your brain to shock it into revival.

So, when a patient goes through all this, you know how serious the condition is, and how much suffering is involved in having depression.

But there is also a natural way to cure depression. In this process there is no suffering if all the steps outlined is followed through by the patient.

First of all, the patient's body needs to be de-toxified, by this I mean for any period between 9 months to 12 months, the food intake of the patient is self-controlled, he is advised to reduce his weight, by naturally consuming fruits and salads only with milk during this period. He has to main this diet for this period. The body is filled with energy in this process, as it is shocked out of malnutrition and all diseases. While this is going on, the patient needs to practice Yoga and Dhyana (Meditation) on a daily basis throughout this period. This special type of Yoga, leads to activation of the chakras, with Kundalini awakening, these are energy centres, which are activated from the pelvic area to the top of your head, there are 7 such chakras, and when energy flows from these chakras, from the bottom to the top, your consciousness is awakened, and you become self-aware, and come to know about the true nature of your existence, as you also meditate daily as part of your Yoga daily schedule.

During the same period, you are advised to follow a celibate life during this period, this helps gaining control of the hormones releases in your body system, which helps the brain to recover and yanks it out of its lethargy to alertness. This also must continue for 12 months curing period.

After 12 months of this practice, you will find a transformation in yourself and your personality, as you come out completely cured, and full of energy, and enthusiasm for life, and with a capability and zeal to work and support yourself.

You have been cured of depression, the Yoga and Dhyana suggested, is best learnt from the Isha foundation of Sadhguru Jaggi Vasudevji. Which will give the fastest and best results to reach normalcy and balance in life.

Two more suggestion are important to follow, you can eat normal sensible diet, but keep at least 40% of your food intake daily of fruits and salads, to maintain health and vitality.

Secondly, as far as your celibacy is concerned, you may continue it, till you marry, and want to have children, and you return to celibacy to assume the responsibility of your children, leading a celibate life.

Celibacy or bramacharya is an open secret to all success in your life, and if you want your life to be full of accomplishments!

You look forward to living a wonderful life ahead, with your family, after your curing from depression is over and you assume responsibility in life as a normal person! God bless you!

Chapter 21

Home for the Homeless

The problem of the homeless is very acute in our country. Well, it is to be expected that almost all the families below poverty line itself, comprising of nearly 22% of the population, or 33 crore people live below the poverty line, and their monthly per capita spending is approximately Rs. 1000 or less, they do not have a home, and any access to live a dignified life in our nation. Also, for a large part of the population, though we cannot call homeless, but who live without their own home, but in rented accommodation. They comprise the poor, the below average and the middle class, for whom having their own home is a dream. Since the population of our nation is the second highest in the world, close to 1. 5 Billion, and soon going to be the highest beating China soon, it is a daunting task, firstly to ensure that, the homeless are elevated to living in a home, and those living in rented apartments, fulfil their dream of having their own home.

So then, when such a large chuck of the population is without their own home, what solution can we come up with to see that their dreams are fulfilled? Well, obviously, to make good homes, which are affordable for them and provide them with their own homes. But homes are so costly to make, and it takes lots of time to make them, or are they really? In our modern technologically advanced age of industrialisation? Let me Introduce a new technology or concept in building, good, sturdy, healthy, and beautiful homes: This new technology is known as factory made homes/Modular homes/Prefabricated homes/or Mobile homes. These homes are made in the factory, and are either assembled at the site, or just made and transported in big trucks to the customers and installed at their site. They are made or fabricated primarily from, steel, wood, plastic and glass apart from a few other materials, which are strong, lightweight, have all the modern amenities such as toilets, Washrooms, Electrical connections for lighting and devices, are insulated from the weather, be it rain, cold or the heat of summer, they are termite and pest resistant, and more over the damage from risk of floods or earthquake is very limited and less harmful! And moreover, if you order a mobile home, with a configuration of enhancing your home with portability and mobility, you have the option of shifting your home to a different location, if you want to live in a different place, these homes are such that they are collapsible, and can be transported on trucks, or even by aircraft cargo! And the most outstanding aspect of these modern high-tech homes is, they can be made ready in 15 days from fabrication to installation, and are dirt cheap compared to conventional brick and mortar homes! Standard homes can cost anywhere between 1. 5 lakhs to 5 lakhs to own!

Since they are so much in budget of the public at large, they can be made an alternative to solve the problem of homelessness in India! For those living individuals living below poverty line, they can receive government funding, and all the slums can be cleared in the cities, with them, and this can be an affordable alternative for the rural homelessness and lack of shelter to crores of people living in the villages! With loan provisions, and subsidy from the government, the problem of the poor who are homeless can be solved head on! The best technology for this is available at a cheaper cost in China, with whom we can have a tech tie up! When this activity is scaled up, it can solve the problem, of homelessness in our nation forever!

A home for all, becomes a dream for our nation to accomplish with ease!

Chapter 22

Defining the Future Relationship of the Loving Brothers India & Pakistan

India & Pakistan have been at war over possession of Kashmir for over 77 years now.

We do not need Violence and fighting between brothers anymore.

We are brothers, we belong emotionally to each other and will always do so, as we once were one and shared everything, as common between us as a family.

This bond cannot be broken ever in our future history.

So the basic thing to understand, we need to learn to be kind and caring towards each other, as we are members of one family.

Now coming to the dispute over Kashmir, the solution has to be through peaceful diplomacy, not war or violence.

We wasted 77 years fighting. We do not want to waste any more time or give each other any more suffering. We need to first recognize, that we are own brother's.

So then, the call is to end hostilities now.

And what else? We need to be patient, we need to wait for the right kind of leadership to come to power in India, to take forward the diplomatic process to come to a amicable solution between our two Nations.

Both sides need to realise and trust each other to work out a solution, by negotiations, working out what is more important about Kashmir to both the nations.

I am sure when responsible government takes power, a amicable solution will come about, which may include a pebilisite to be held in Kashmir, with both the nations approval. And a workable and peaceful solution will come.

However, both need to understand, whatever the outcome of the diplomatic and negotiations process, we never forget that we are one family, and we would treat each other with the respect, kindness, caring and love forever as, as one family member does to another.

Moreover, we help each other, in every way, economically, and in every other way, grow with common interest and support each other, including tourism, and facilitate the interaction culturally, heritage, and relationships between each other which have been there between the people of India and Pakistan always.

So this is what is the loving future of brothers India & Pakistan. This applies to Bangladesh also.

May Allah or Mataji bless our family with Peace, Love, Kindness, caring, prosperity and happiness forever.

Chapter 23

Employment for the Unemployed

We are aware of the unemployment scenario in our nation India. Particularly regarding the youth scenario in India, we have the highest proportion of our population of young adults in the world today, and the prevailing situation of large-scale unemployment, is a worry factor for our nation. The unemployment scenario creates lots of frustration in our youth, and it can cause lots of social disturbance, and the youth who are full of energy, can be misled, in the wrong direction, which can cause harm to them or others and can ruin their lives.

As per current figures, there are 31 million unemployed in India; about 4.1% of our population is young and unemployed. And even more worrying there are 35% of the population who are underemployed. Underemployed means, highly skilled workers do not have any appropriate jobs, and are doing menial jobs to make a living. This is abnormal wastage of talent of our youth, who despite having good qualifications, do small labour work, to sustain their subsistence living. This is even more worrisome, as this is disguised unemployment, which is a very huge proportion of the population. This is a very large part of the population, which is acutely frustrated and can cause a lot of social unrest in our society. These categories of people earn even less than the per capita income of India which is 8,000 rupees per month. This is called subsistence living.

There are currently approximately 11 crore Indians who are underemployed in our nation, who are skilled and qualified individuals, who are underemployed! Another glaring statistic is that nearly 8 lakh people, who are highly qualified engineers, are currently underemployed or unemployed! This is terrible waste of our human capital, as well as the resources which were used to skill them! The account of unemployed in the agricultural industry, is even more glaring fact, there are nearly 38 crore Indians who are underemployed and frustrated and making a meagre subsistence living in the rural areas, who do menial work to survive in the agricultural sector of India!

For the unemployed, and underemployed of India, this is a hopeless situation, and it is very easy to understand, why and how they fall prey, and are recruited by the anti-social elements, in our society, and exploited by them, and the resultant high crime rate of India we witness today!

So, then what is the solution to this? Well, first an unemployment registrar needs to be created in our nation, and the details of all of them needs to be registered with the government of India. With their identity records created, in the same step, during the same process is, to capture their skills and educational records as their unemployment records are generated.

Well, we do have a large part of our population, gainfully employed also. And in our society, there is a very disturbing imbalance of income and wealth in our society, as we all know. The rich get richer, the poor the poorer! India's top 1% of the population, bag or account for 73% of India's wealth. This is very unfortunate for our nation. Another anomaly of our economy is that less than 3% of the population are income tax payers in our nation. Whereas in other countries such as USA, UK, Japan, Etc.

the percentage of population paying taxes are above 50% of the population.

These are all abnormal and worrying statistics of our nation. In developed economies the major portion of the government revenues come from income tax, whereas for our nation the major share comes from indirect taxes.

Another important point to note, in developed economies, the unemployed are guaranteed employment as per law, so when an individual is unemployed there, till he gets employed, he gets unemployment benefits from the government, as soon as he registers himself as unemployed with government authorities. And as per law, the burden of the unemployed is carried by those who are employed, and this burden is collected or deducted from the revenue coming from the income tax paid by them to the government, till the time the unemployed are gainfully employed and absorbed in the economy.

We in India, need a law such as the one followed in developed countries, first all unemployed need to be registered with the government, with their current qualifications and skills mapped,, and at least the minimum wages, as unemployment benefits need to be paid to all such individuals, who are unemployed in our nation. That amounts to Rs. 176 per day or Rs. 5,456 per month, if not more. Ideally the minimum wages threshold needs to go up, to Rupees 8,000 per month which is ideal to exist with minimum dignity as a human being. This amount needs to be paid, to all registered unemployed in our nation, till they are gainfully employed.

But then the question comes about funding such a step in the right direction, the needs for funding can only come from indirect taxes revenues, as direct tax revenues collected are negligible as income taxes. There can be a 3 pronged approach to funding this vital activity, firstly, as we know there is inequality in our economy which is of an alarming proportion, so the items consumed by the rich class needs to be taxed with a highest rate, to garner revenues, we need to create a luxury scale of measurement of items available for sale in the market, be it anything, based on the points scored on luxurious spending, we need to tax high, those items we identify as superfluous consumption purchased for a luxurious life style. Secondly, we can tax items which people consume, which are generally considered a health hazard, Tobacco based, chewing or smoking all types of liquor, and Gutkas. Thirdly, we need to see that we do not burden any basic items of consumption especially that which is consumed by the middle class and poor class of our society. This way three objectives are achieved at the same time- curbing the consumption of intoxicants, and health hazards, second helping reduce inequality in society, and thirdly, creating a safety net for the unemployed and underemployed of Bharat, and creation of employment opportunities for them.

Another good step would be to take low interest loans from the IMF and World Bank to fund large infrastructure spending,andforfinancingprojectssuchascreationofschools, colleges, and hospitals under government management of the top quality on the model we see in developed economies of the world, for creation of employment opportunities in Bharat.

Some further data regarding the labour situation in our Bharat: Regarding Labour Participation Rate & Work Force Deployment, I wish to once again draw attention to the following facts:

The Labour participation Rate in our nation is currently best at 50% of the population of our country.

However, in comparison, the Labour Participation Rate as a ratio of Total population is nothing less than 70% to 91% in Most of the Advanced Economies Currently. Especially in Saudi Arabia, Japan, UK & North America.

This gives us an idea, about the productive population in our nation. The more the % of Labour participating in the work force, the less the burden on the working population, to feed the unemployed and the underemployed. Moreover, this also indicates, the absolute non-involvement of a major part of our work force, which is also the defining factor about the underlying reasons for the high rate of poverty and crime in our nation.

Below, I present further statistics on Labour Participation Rate in our nation:

Labour Participation ratios: (PER 1,000 Population Ratio), as per year 2011–12 data available on Niti Ayog Website: All India: 460

Male: 558

Female: 253.

India Rural: Male: 553 Female: 253

All Rural: 406

India Urban: Male 563 Female: 253

All Urban: 367.

Of this effective working population, the deployment of work force as per industry is as under:

(PER 1,000 Population Ratio).

1. Rural Overall:

Agriculture: 641 Of these females: 749, Males: 599.

Mining & Quarry: 5 Of these females: 2. 9 Males: 5

Manufacturing: 86 of these females: 98 Males: 81

Construction 94 Females: 66 Males: 130

Electricity, Gas, Water Supply: 2 Females '0' Males 3

Trade (Whole sale & Retail): 14 Females: 30 Males: 80

Transportation, Storage & Communication: 30 Females 2 Males: 42

Public Administration & Community Service: 53 Females: 50 Males: 54

Finance & Insurance Services: 8 Females: 2 Males: 7 Urban Overall:

Agriculture: 67 Females 109 Males 60

Mining & Quarry: 236 Females: 3 Males 9

An active monitoring needs to be done on the registered unemployed to reduce their number, by creating employment opportunities for them. This is only about the unemployed, the problem of the underemployed is also acute, and the economy of the nation, needs to be boosted by either government spending towards creation of employment, or by releasing both fiscal, monetary and budgetary policies to fuel the economic growth of the nation, and direct creation of employment opportunities in our nation, in an accelerated mode.

This is the minimum we can expect from our government of India as bold policy initiatives towards the compensation and creation of employment opportunities in our nation, to allow each citizen of our nation live a minimum dignified life.

Chapter 24

Reforming the Judicial System of India

In our country the judicial system is based on the British System, and changes have been made in this system, time to time to suit our Indian Scenario.

The hierarchy of both the civil courts and criminal courts is like this, the highest is the Supreme court, then below the State courts at state level, and then below them, the Metropolitan courts, and the District Courts and Session Courts.

The main problems with the current system are:

Firstly, too many pending cases, piling up both in civil and criminal courts, the litigations are marred by delays, on an abnormal time scale, to the extent, that it becomes a case of Justice denied to the aggrieved party. Time for pronouncement of Judgement stretches to decades, this is criminal neglect, and due to this more crimes or litigations are perpetuated, from lack of fear of persecution. Which means in the courts, illegal proceedings are going on, aimed towards blocking or denying Justice, and this is the true state of affairs for the citizens of India, Justice is marred in most cases!

A deliberate attempt by the party, to deny justice to the aggrieved party, by constantly pushing the proceedings, into the timeless Scenario, since cases are not time bound, means the accused goes Scott free.

Solution: First new laws to be made to prevent deliberate attempts to delay proceedings unduly. It should be made a criminal offence and punishment to be given to the accused, for any such attempts.

Both Civil cases and Criminal cases Judgement should be time bound, to a maximum of 30 days. Any deviation from this should need sanction from first the High court, up to another 15 days, and sanction for judgement after 45 days to 60 days must need Supreme court sanction.

This is the only way, Justice can be imparted, with Judgement pronounced, and our present Judicial system can be reformed and made effective in India.

There are two more issues regarding criminal courts, one, Wrong Judgement Given, Second, Judgement given not imparted or implemented.

Solution: When wrong judgement is given, relief through appeal to Higher courts and due diligence by a appointed Jury, again Time bound.

For Judgement not implemented, appeal to higher courts with punishment to the accused, again time bound.

With these steps our Judicial system will be effective, and Justice will be given to aggrieved party and not denied, respecting the constitution of India.

God bless our Judiciary!

Chapter 25

Akhand Bharat

As we look at the history of our Indian Subcontinent, it is but obvious that Bharat was much bigger. And our India of today, is part of the bigger Indian subcontinent, and the Indian area of Influences, Cultural commonality, religious commonality, our way of living, our food, etc... Is similar to the other nations which broke away from the Original Bharat or you can also call it Hindustan. We have the same heritage, connected History together, the attire, music, and the arts, the languages etc.. A lot which is common.

For example, Nepal, Burma, Bhutan, Maldives, Mauritius, Thailand, Malaysia, Indonesia, the Philippines, Bangladesh, Pakistan, Singapore, Tibet, SriLankan, Afghanistan..., to take the major areas of Influence, and not to Mention India at the Centre of it all?.

You will find same type of Temples, Food, Archi structure, religious practices, festivals, monuments, languages, currency, ancient texts, festivals a common psychology in the Indian Subcontinent.

With so much in common, should we not unite, over a common purpose, with a multi-national ALLAINCE, where we serve our common interests in the region, enriching the lives of people population all these nations? Starting with tourism, educational exchanges, cultural exchanges, sharing each other heritage, festivals, economic cooperation, Business promotions, Military, student programs, NO visa required, or Visa on Arrival etc...

As nations we may have our own entity, like in the European union, or the EU. The EU is a good model to emulate. They have a common currency, no visa required, complete one business market, etc...

Why can't we use the EU as a Model to Emulate? It is the best one. I am sure all the nations stand to gain from each other, for mutual benefit.

Iam sure this will be beautiful & wonderful to do this for all the nations!

I am suggesting a grand name for this National Alliance, in the Indian Subcontinent: Akhand Bharat! It is similar to the European Union, and our Akhand Bharat will be a great power Centre, just like the European Union, is now! A power Centre to envy and recon with!

May Mataji Bless Akhand Bharat!

Thank You!

www.ingramcontent.com/pod-product-compliance
Lightning Source LLC
Chambersburg PA
CBHW051058250726
48656CB00001B/361